Shifting PARADIGMS

ISBN-13: 978-1500969059
ISBN-10: 1500969052

Shifting

PARADIGMS

Table of Contents

Chapter 1 – What is a paradigm shift?

All people are products of their genetic tendencies as modified through their experiences in their environments. People learn culture and social norms through institutional conditioning by parents, schools, media and government. Social norms cause people to seek external validation through social interactions and expectations through which they define the value of others and their own self-worth. Social conditioning "boxes" allows people to define their niche and place in society as categorized by government and stereotypes perpetuated by mass media and group thinkers. Consequently people see reflections of themselves in their family and social roes, careers, job titles, economic class, race, sex/gender, sexual preference, religion and political and religious perspectives. This book explores many of the institutionalized, political, philosophical, cultural, economic and social "boxes" where people find comfort and security in knowing where they belong in the larger scheme of things. But do their personal boxes truly define who they are, or does it generally act to limit their potential development as if seeing the Earth as the center of the universe when the universe surrounds us all. Incremental social changes are generational in nature and solidly rooted attitudes are difficult to change and become institutionalized or become an unexplainable tradition. People grow up with a set of preordained assumptions that form their core beliefs from which they become attached to the exclusion of new information, protecting their mental and emotional turf with guarded necessity.

Few people dare to venture out of their personal boxes for fear of criticism, failure, discomfort, uncertainty and possible danger. Most people wouldn't know where to begin even if they should decide to take social risks and to question their true inner needs and beliefs in respect to existing paradigms of thought, speech and behaviors that are acceptable to society. As generation drift occurs to change various aspects of society at large, paradigm shifts occur that essentially replace the old with the new, forcing those whose boxes have provided comfort to either fortify, repair, expand or abandon their personal space in consideration of redefinitions and changes in the social order and its values, rewards and punishments.

When we look at the evolution of culture, political systems, social norms and economic systems, paradigm shifts appear to occur at an unpredictable pace with unforeseen consequences, except to separate the leaders from the followers, the wealthy from the poor, the powerful from the relatively powerless, the manipulators from the manipulated, the shepherds from the sheep. This dualistic bifurcation of societies appears to be a man made consequence of the fittest predators feeding on the game, and the apex predators ruling the world. In terms of human societies, the power paradigm is likely the consequence of natural selection, or survival of the fittest.

During the age of empires, imperialism, colonialism, slavery, rape and pillage that routinely ravaged lands for thousands of years, the apex predators sent their armies to invade other nations and to ransack them, taking control of the spoils of war, including its land, natural resources and peoples. Subsequent to World War 2, the philosophical perspective of global leaders turned to a paradigm of pacification, reserving warfare as its supposed last resort through false flag justifications that preserved their power. Economic and political power had to appear as legitimate to assure the global elites that the system of things that gave them rule would not become threatened or destroyed by anarchy.

Similar to the animal kingdom where predators are at the top of the food chain wait or sneak around for opportunities to attack their prey, human predators essentially utilize similar tactics. Apex predators never expose their true intentions and operate in secrecy, thereby allowing their prey to be lulled into a false feeling of security and business as usual. Human predators have created a system of laws to protect their need for secrecy, deception and manipulation of the system to institutionalize their advantages and benefits to the detriment of the populace. We begin this discussion of paradigm shifts with a brief review of the importance of secrecy and the role it serves to maintain the elitist status quo.

The world operates on various principles and presumptions that support specific standards of behavior, interaction and institutionalized paradigms that maintain secrecy, power, elitism, wealth, and social/cultural norms and beliefs. Creating shifts in paradigms can occur relatively suddenly as with the introduction of new technologies or political regimes, or it can happen over generations as with religious, cultural or philosophical ideas that create new social standards and mandates.

THE IMPENDING PARADIGM SHIFTS IN THE WORLD ORDER

Kuhn's notion of paradigms and "paradigm shift" is a concept that has increasing gained academic acceptance in modern times. In past eras, old knowledge was changed and often replaced by new discoveries, even as religious and political institutions attempted to repress non-status quo ideas by outlawing or making such new concepts subjects of blasphemy. Eventually, scientific facts began to outweigh traditional religious explanations of the universe, both known and unknown. What was once defined and finite became less obvious and expansive. At the beginning of the 20th Century, the automobile, airplane, and assembly line, within a relatively short span of 50 years, gave way to supersonic jets, rockets and missiles. Less than ten years later, the Soviet Union began a new era of space exploration. The dawning of the new millennium was met not with the greatly feared catastrophicY2K meltdown, but with new technologies on all fronts of human achievement, many still shrouded in secrecy.

Secrecy is routine government policy. Who really killed JFK, MLK, and RFK? What's the truth about Roswell, Area 51, Aurora, UFOS, and secret weapons? The facts are shrouded in secrecy. On the topic of political assassinations, conspiracy theories abound that run contrary to the government's official "lone gunman" accounts. In the area of UFOs and secret military projects, public inquires are always met with denials or meteorological explanations, or rejected based upon concerns for national security requirements. The full factual stories continue to be shrouded in secrecy. Historically, secrecy has been an essential strategic element of the power paradigm from the beginnings of human civilization.

The power paradigm is one of several paradigms that both determine and explain the realities of institutionalized suppositions that are accepted as real world relationships. The power paradigm comprises the aggregate perceptions based upon supporting paradigms expressed in terms of economic, military, political, technological, scientific, environmental, land-natural resources, and religious power. When several interdependent and interdisciplinary paradigms interact concurrently during a specific period in the evolution of human civilizations, especially as the global economic, political, cultural, and military order becomes more centralized, paradigm shifts are expected, and may be inevitable.

Before Thomas Kuhn created jargon to explain conceptual and perceptual organizational changes on a systemic level, things just changed, became assimilated into existing environments, or exposed new explanations for explaining reality. The world was flat, and then it became round. Europe and other empires thought they were the center of the world, only later to discover they were just another passing fad in the sand of time. The earth was the center of the universe, and then it became an insignificant little speck in the boundless sea of the cosmology. There were many Gods, and then there was the ONE, among a few. Royalty and empires gave way to the power of the people, yet new wealth and power bestowed upon manipulators of the masses simultaneously exploited the miserable condition of impoverished majority, and comparatively, did little to change there overall lot, as the rich continued to get richer at the expense of the worker classes.

These were all paradigm shifts, many of which were contingent and interdependently timed shifts, that otherwise could not have occurred. Knowledge begets knowledge. Were the wheel never invented, the all-polluting automobile, as we know it, could have never existed. Were fire never discovered and harnessed in a reproducible form, we wouldn't have family barbeques. But what if neither the wheel nor fire were ever harnessed? Perhaps we might have had flying cars utilizing anti-gravity propulsion and solar power ovens eons ago. Just perhaps we may not have such a polluted world. As so called paradigm shifts occur, it both advances, and limits knowledge and discovery because it changes the elitist, and thus the majoritarian direction of civilizations. Sometimes, paradigm shifts inhibit human progress. Sometimes it advances humanitarian causes. Usually, it serves the status quo's desire to retain dominance.

Historically, paradigm shifts have been caused by transformative advances in technology, religion, philosophy, political systems, trade, monetary exchange, financial schemes, institutionalized education, and media that have created broad changes to societies, both intentional and unexpected. The effect of paradigm shifts has had widespread social, cultural, political, religious, and economic outcomes over time.

The Cost Benefits of Secrecy

What is meant by secrecy? Why do people and organizations feel compelled to have secrets? Secrecy is defined in the book <u>Right and Responsibilities of Participants in Networked Communities</u> (Denning & Lin, 1994: 40) as activities designed to prevent "deliberate disclosures of information to individuals not authorized to receive that information. The information kept secret may refer to contents of a message... or to the identity of a message's author...." Who benefits from secrecy? And who benefits from exposing or stealing secrets? In so far as how secrecy applies to technology, and how technology has impacted the ability to safeguard secrets, an examination of four sectors of society that regularly practice secrecy should be examined: government (political and bureaucratic) or state secrecy; military secrecy; corporate (business) secrecy; and criminal secrecy.

As technology has made information flow instantaneous, pervasive, and readily available, the ability of organizations to keep *secrets* secret is being assailed on all fronts. Cyber terrorism is a new term that didn't exist more than a decade ago. The attack on secrecy can be made on many fronts, using varied tactics and technologies; consequently organizations and institutions are taking exceptional steps to safeguard their secrets.

On August 16-18, 1999, approximately 40 researchers and government research sponsors involved with information system security met at RAND, Santa Monica CA, to address and recommend technical research and development initiatives focused on mitigating the insider threat. It has become widely acknowledged that "insider misuse" is one of the greatest threats to, and obstacles in achieving "information assurance" within critical Defense information systems (RAND, 2001). In recognition of this, an Integrated Process Team developed a strategy to help identify and respond to cyber espionage from the "insider threat".

In an effort to hunt for potential secret terrorists, law enforcement officials at Super Bowl XXXV in Tampa secretly scanned spectators' faces with surveillance cameras and instantly compared their "face prints" against those of suspected terrorists and known criminals in a computerized database. Alarmed civil libertarians quickly raised the specter of a Big Brother government spying on its citizens. But is the growing use of this technology cause for alarm? Is it an undesirable invasion of individual privacy, or does it represent a positive advance in security measures that generates benefits for society? (Woodward, 2001).

Technology has made both guarding secrets a more difficult task, and stealing secrets a more accessible and less detectable option;

consequently, technology is being called upon to provide more effective safeguards to ensuring secrecy of all types, by all segments of society. Secrecy of civilian governments invariably cause the public to ask, "What do they want to hide and why do they want to hide it? Political corruption, collusion, and conspiracies have proven to become the focus of scandalous media coverage, where even the private sexual conduct of an American President takes the nation down the path of impeachment. The nature of our bi-partisan federalist system of government creates a competitive polity where individuals struggle against others in advancing their personal (and party's) causes, goals, and agendas.

Another primary motivator for state secrecy is to avoid the disclosure of information that might lead to mass panic, potential rebellion, and anarchy. Consequently, cover-up of mistakes and misdeeds by the nation's political and economic elites serve to legitimize government and to maintain social, political, and economic stability that is thought to be requisites for domestic and global peace. Despite this state agenda, according to a longitudinal National Election Study, a majority of American voters do not trust the federal government to do right (NES, 1996).

A report by the Milken Institute explained that the Federal Reserve's current practice, unlike many central banks, is for relatively opaque and secretive policy-making, remarking, "It has never clearly articulated precise policy goals to Congress or to the public" and relies on secrecy in our political system (Milken, 2001). The United States, being the world's remaining super power, is subject to attack on many fronts, both domestically and around the world. The Oklahoma Bombing, the bombing of the U.S. Destroyer Cole in the Persian Gulf, and bombings of U.S. Embassies in Africa are clear examples of danger that American citizens, interests, and property face daily at home and abroad.

In order to maintain a military advantage and deterrence to our real and potential adversaries, whether they are nations, organization, or terrorist groups, America's military conducts extensive secret research and development to enable our nation to fight both current and future wars.

Since WW2, the military-industrial complex actively engages in the development of secret weapons in a multitude of scientific disciplines; including space, nuclear, genomic, viral, meteorological, nanotechnology; biotechnology; Internet, surveillance, mind-control, biochip implants, holography, and pharmacological, just to name a few (Shadowlands, 2001).

For example, according to Persinger (1995), subharmonic patterns in naturally occurring or technically generated magnetic fields affect all brains which operate within certain ranges of inaudible Extra-Low Frequency waves (ELFs). One of the primary uses of ELFs is to communicate with submarines, as ELFs go right through the earth and, of course, right through metal walls. But researchers have also found that frequency waves below 6 cycles per second cause people to become very emotionally upset, and even disrupts bodily functions. At 8.2 cycles, people can be made to feel very high, and 11 to 11.3 cycles induces agitation leading to riotous behavior.

Dr. Puharich (1984) revealed that the Soviets used ELF waves to experiment with weather control in 1976 and 1977, using an 11 Hertz wave sent around the world; but even when they stopped their transmitters, they couldn't stop the waves! It took a year for the 11 Hertz wave to diminish in strength, causing a terrible winter. Since the Russians turned on this signal, they have had three crop failures in a row, as well as great floods. America had great heat and drought. Are incidents of continuing violence around the world related to secret ELF emissions?

Many examples abound to what extent corporations attempt to protect their secrets. Tobacco company deceptions, when exposed, subjected them to untold hundreds of millions of dollars in civil monetary penalties to settle individual and class action litigation. The federal government continues its anti-trust investigation of Microsoft, with industry leaders demanding public disclosure of their proprietary source code on the justification that Microsoft had used its company secrets to create a monopoly. More recently, Lucent Technology is pursuing individuals for alleged theft of their company's trade secrets that may cause them future irreparable economic harm. The courts have weighed in on the side of trade secrets, for example in the case of Sega Enterprises vs. Accolade Inc., issues of copyright and trademark infringement were upheld by the U.S. Supreme Court (Huerta, 2001). The Sega case demonstrates the importance of secrecy in maintaining competitive advantage. In that case, Accolade had reverse engineered products based upon Sega's codes to gain market share.

As the economies of the world continue to become more global and interdependent, the competitive advantages that nations and corporations attempt to attain has increased commensurately. Secrecy also decreases the probability of effective external threats or attacks. In the case of The United States vs. Robert Morris, a graduate student who developed an Internet virus was convicted for causing damage by uploading it to military, government and university computer networks (Huerta, 2001). Secrecy helps to control the proliferation of potentially dangerous technologies or critical information, as shown by the case of Armstrong vs. the President of the United States of America, where an agency head responsible for record keeping for the executive office was found guilty of failures that resulted in the destruction of irrecoverable federal electronic data (Huerta, 2001).

Governments tend to attach the catchall excuse for secrecy; "for national security reasons." RAND (2001) observed that the high cost of military cryptography makes it extremely difficult to ensure secrecy in military transmissions. They state that secrecy in attempting to protect the spread of new developments in a ripe technology does not afford true blanket security because highly technically trained people are usually able to construct essential aspects of secrets through unclassified information. Technology makes information more easily accessible to manipulation. Computing devices and silicon technology continues to improve at a pace that doubles the number of transistors per chip every 18-24 months.

Consequently, today's microprocessors operate at almost 2 Gigahertz, but by the year 2011, a 10 Gigahertz rate is expected. The Cray supercomputer in 1988 cost about $14 Million; today, that same performance is expected from a Pentium III that cost under $1,000. These quantum technological advances made available for anyone at minimal cost provide advanced platforms for conducting attacks against institutional secrets, which forces governments to create more secrets.

Vulnerability of macro-systems to attacks was addressed by RAND (2001) in a hypothetical scenario that demonstrated the potential catastrophe that could be cause by multi-prong cyber attacks on the military and civilian computer and telecommunications infrastructure of the U.S.A. Vulnerability of pervasive technologies toward massive, uncontrollable, and unpredictable failures with potentially dire consequences is a theme advanced by Adams (1998:17), who explained that information warfare breaks down into three distinct pieces: perception management where information is the message, systems destruction where information is the medium, and information exploitation where information is an opponent's resource to be targeted. Just how difficult would it be to cripple telecommunications and data systems on four continents by taking out one FLAG cable? FLAG is the Fiber-Optic Link Around the Globe that crosses the South Pacific, Asia, the Middle East, and the North Atlantic that will eventually pass through Alexandria, Egypt. Clearly a strategically placed bomb could cause havoc with global communications (Adams, 1998: 173).

Adams described an incident in 1990, when a tiny glitch in some AT&T software which the company sent to all its switching centers brought the entire system to a halt for nine hours. He concludes that when software is standardized across a multitude of platforms, be it at a corporate or national level, the lack of redundancy creates a large degree of vulnerability (Adams, 1998:173). When Bank of America employees were conducting "routine maintenance on half of an electrical substation the bank operates at a data processing center, a worker accidentally shut off power to the on-line unit, one switch that disabled 40 percent of the bank's ATMs (Adams, 1998:174).

Corporate economic interests often require it to keep secret its financial arrangements, trade secrets, and other proprietary information. Failure to do so permits potential competitors to steal secrets of industrial or technological processes, key technical and executive employees, and to determine other strategic weaknesses that may be attacked for competitive gain. Political survivalists require the avoidance of scandals, stigma, and penalties that would otherwise destroy their political effectiveness or careers. With today's pervasive Internet capabilities, you can find out practically anything about a person and/or business. An employer touting the Cyber Detective software claimed they routinely use it to screen new employees before hiring, discovered an applicant wanted by the FBI for embezzlement was applying for a job in their accounting department (EzDetective, 2001). These tools can now be used to snoop on politicians, CEOs, or any potential or real political enemy.

Nation-states typically spend a great portion of their budgets on protecting and ensuring systems survival against real and potential enemies, both domestic and foreign. A study by RAND's Lesser & Hoffman (2001) points to the need for the United States to formulate a clear, realistic, and realizable national strategy that can evolve with the changing terrorist threat. Four core elements to that strategy emphasized reducing systemic causes, deterring terrorists and their sponsors, reducing the risk of "super terrorism" such as attacks involving weapons of mass destruction, and retaliating where deterrence fails. They conclude, "With its increasing lethality, possible access to weapons of mass destruction, and the shift to flexible and robust network organization, terrorism is a more formidable problem than ever before. Air and space power will be critical elements in defending U.S. interests-including USAF forces-against this evolving threat." (Lesser, Hoffman, 2001).

Criminals and criminal organizations have always required the cover of secrecy to conduct their illegal business. In 1902, Adam Worth was considered the greatest thief of "modern times" because he had reportedly stolen $3,000,000 over several decades (Macintyre, 1997: viii-ix). In our "modern times", illegally obtained international loot is secretly laundered to offshore banks by criminals, corrupt public officials, and terrorist states. Economic competitors seem to lurk at every turn, consequently, individuals and businesses attempt to obtain legal protection before their trade secrets could be safely made public. In the case Diamond v. Chakrabarty decided on June 16, 1980, the U.S. Supreme Court found that creation of a bacterium that is not found anywhere in nature, constituted a patentable manufacture or "composition of matter", moreover, the bacterium's man-made ability to break down crude oil made it very useful and patentable. To further protect trade secrets, the U.S. Congress passed the Economic Espionage Act of 1996 (Public Law 104-294), defining "economic espionage" as an offense that will benefit any foreign government, foreign instrumentality, or foreign agent.

Political enmities keep the national news corps in business. Infamous secrets became scandals that cost politicians their reputations and even their careers. Watergate, Iran-gate, and Monica-gate, had the collateral effect of dozens of political resignations. It seems Washington D.C. is a tough place to keep a secret. Enemies of the state abound. RAND's Lesser & Hoffman (2001) concluded that counter terrorism today requires diverse responses to an increasingly diverse challenge. In addition to becoming more lethal, the terrorist threat is changing in another dimension as well as one driven by computer and communication networks. The most striking development here is not attacks on America's information infrastructure, but destruction may present a new and deadlier threat. High-tech weapons and nuclear materials from the former Soviet Union are increasingly available, and chemical or biological warfare agents are easily manufactured. Amateurs in particular, who may be exploited or manipulated by professional terrorists or covert sponsors, may be willing to use these weapons (Lesser & Hoffman, 2001).

Criminal enterprises have become more sophisticated. In 1902, stealing $3 Million made Adam Worth the greatest thief at that time. By this new millennium, the Russian Mafiya had already pulled off the largest jewelry heist, insurance, and Medicare frauds in American history, with a net haul exceeding $1 billion. Russian President Boris Yeltsin described Russia as "the biggest Mafia state in the world" and "the superpower of crime." (Friedman, 2000: xix). When the CIA was asked in 1992 to help located $20 billion that was hidden offshore by the KGB and the mob, the Bush national security policy team declined to cooperate (Friedman, 2000: 263). Instead, with the vigorous support of the United States, another $20 billion of IMF loans was deposited directly into Russia's Central Bank (Friedman, 2000: 263).

Is *Knowledge*, the *Forbidden Fruit*? According to the Bible, God cast the first humans out of heaven for eating from the *Tree of Knowledge of Good and Bad*. What knowledge might be threatening to humans, and perhaps should remain secret? What are the short and long term implications and potential consequences of technological advances in genomics, cloning, propulsion technology, biotechnology, and nanotechnology? No one can predict the unexpected outcomes that may either advance humanity, or send us back to the stone age or into extinction. Secrecy can be an effective tool to maintain society's stability. How would people handle the disclosure of irrefutable facts that would debunk past state secrets about such matters as UFOs, political assassinations, and secret experimentation on an unsuspecting populace? What if it could be proven that a secret world government exists, and that the new world order strategy calls for the elimination of two-thirds of the world's population through AIDS and other manmade diseases?

Government elites typically don't believe that common people are either educated enough or sufficiently rational and emotionally stable to handle information that runs contrary to their religious or cultural beliefs. Secrecy may be required for people to continue living in their daily survival mode; otherwise, the consequences of knowing too much may be dangerous to people's outlook on life, and could potentially cause chaos.

Steve Jobs, co-founder of Apple Computer, commenting on a new technological device, stated, "If enough people see the machine you won't have to convince them to architect cities around it. It'll just happen." According to (Mark, 2001), Jobs was referring to "IT", also code-named Ginger, an invention developed by 49-year-old scientist Dean Kamen. "IT" is so extraordinary that it has drawn the attention of technology visionaries Jeff Bezos and Steve Jobs and the investment dollars of pre-eminent Silicon Valley venture capitalist John Doerr. This new invention supposedly will sweep over the world and change lives, cities, and ways of thinking, and its core technology and applications will, have a profound impact on social institutions and some billion-dollar old-line companies (Mark, 2001). Who knows, since Apples are computers, maybe Dean Kamen has found a way to make pigs fly. Update: the expected revolutionary erect biped vehicle marketed as the "Segway" has not caused the envisioned change to populace transportation over a decade later, perhaps due to its steep $5,000+ unit price and its inherent instability despite its reliance on gyros that don't prevent a tip over that resulted in the unexpected death of Segway's CEO, Jimi Heselden who fell over a bridge and drowned in the river below.

The Balance Between Secrecy and Openness

Is Mankind really kind? Or does reflecting on the experiences of our own lives, confirmed by media, literature, and history books indicate that human beings in general are prone to deception, dishonesty, disagreement, and other common practices that are untrustworthy? Secrecy may be essential to human survival. Secrets kept about sexual indiscretions keep marriages intact, so dependent children may benefit from a stable home environment. It is usually after secrets become exposed that marital strife begins. The public often hears about murders relating to lovers spats when secret lovers are disclosed, which have even become the mainstay of late night television. Today, easy access to communication and spy technology permits encroachment on and exposure of previously undetectable secrets, and as a result, the arenas of conflict are certain to increase. Society may no longer be able to call upon secrecy to be its social pressure safety valve.

The federal Freedom of Information Act has created a new set of threats to state and trade secrets, such that NASA is unable to properly protect intellectual property, which becomes disclosed to the public and is available to all companies, foreign and domestic. (Rand, 2001). Ramifications and repercussions from exposure of secrets are uncertain, and are generally detrimental to the entity that possessed the secrets. The public desire for increased government transparency does not necessarily assure more responsive or better governance. Congressional and local government meetings are regularly broadcasted on television, and does not appear to make for better government. The free for all on the information highway, the Internet, has created a medium where confidential data is routinely misused, pilfered, redirected, and subterfuge for illegal objectives

Complete openness and lack of secrecy is not the solution to world problems. What if there were no such things as secrets? I surmise the intuitively exploitive nature of the human species would increase conflict due to its natural aggression and destructive tendencies. What if xeno-transplantations (transplantation of body parts from one species to a different species) could be improved, aided by attempts to genetically modify donor tissue and organ antibodies, and regulatory proteins to reduce or eliminate rejection? Baboons or pigs, for example, may be genetically modified and cloned to produce organs for human transplant, although large-scale success may not occur by 2015 (Anton, 2001). But once humans can do that, they would likely engineer baboons to be surrogate mothers for human fetuses so women can be as equal as men, and not have to take off from work to give birth. The greater cosmetic advantages of not having to develop stretch marks from pregnancies will permit women to keep their trim thong figures. This would be a huge paradigm shift to free women from the burdens of pregnancies to permit them to pursue uninterrupted careers as men generally enjoy.

Anton (2001) warns "In the early part of the 21st century, the technologies emerging from the information technology and biotechnology revolutions will present unprecedented governance challenges to national and international political systems. These technologies are now shifting and will continue to affect the organization of society and the ways in which norms emerge and governance structures operate." Anton (2001) predicts that life in 2015 will be revolutionized by the growing effect of multidisciplinary technology across all dimensions of life: social, economic, political, and personal. Biotechnology will enable us to identify, understand, manipulate, improve, and control living organisms (including ourselves). The revolution of information availability and utility will continue to profoundly affect the world in all these dimensions. Smart materials, agile manufacturing, and nanotechnology will change the way we produce devices while expanding their capabilities. The results could be astonishing. Effects may include significant improvements in human quality of life and life span, high rates of industrial turnover, lifetime worker training, continued globalization, reshuffling of wealth, cultural amalgamation or invasion with potential for increased tension and conflict, shifts in power from nation states to non-governmental organizations and individuals, mixed environmental effects, improvements in quality of life with accompanying prosperity and reduced tension, and the possibility of human eugenics and human cloning. Update: Recently, biotechnologists claim that full body transplants utilizing new micro surgical procedures could within a few years permit the successful transplantation of human heads to donor bodies. The shift in paradigm on how people view life and death, and possible immortality would be revolutionary.

However, he (Anton, 2001) adds acceleration of human-engineered evolution of plants, animals, and in some ways even humans with accompanying changes in the ecosystem presents challenges and unforeseeable risks. Research is also under way to create new, free-living organisms. Despite these potentials, Anton (2001) predicts continuing controversy over such issues as eugenics; cloning of humans (including concerns over morality, errors, induced medical problems, gene ownership, and human breeding); gene patents; the safety and ethics of genetically modified organisms; concerns over animal rights brought about by transplantation from animals as well as the risk of trans-species disease; privacy of genetic profiles; the danger of environmental havoc from genetically modified organisms, and an increased risk of engineered biological weapons. I interpret Anton's concerns to implicate the potential total collapse of civilizations and possible extinction of the human species on earth.

Keeping Secrets

Let's consider some age-old clichés about secrecy. *Everyone has secrets...* would you like to know mine? But if I were to tell, it would no longer be a secret. Curiosity is an inherited human trait, a survival instinct from infancy, without which humans could have never landed on the moon, or developed nuclear weapons. Question is, was satisfying our curious nature worth the potential outcomes? If only the walls could talk. What would they say? Walls have absorbed the sound waves emanating from people over the decades. Perhaps all the wisdom and knowledge is now locked in the molecules and atoms that comprise walls. Things said or done behind closed doors were once secrets. Now, new spy technologies readily bought over the counter allow even amateur snoopy neighbors to listen to your secret conversations, record your moves with night vision cameras, intercept your private emails, and even get naked photos of unsuspecting people in changing rooms, restrooms, or motel rooms. Coming out of the closet (or in this case, when a phone booth gets too hot). In the case of Katz v. United States, decided on December 18, 1967, acting on a suspicion that Katz was transmitting gambling information over the phone to clients in other states, federal agents attached an eavesdropping device to the outside of a public phone booth used by Katz. The Court decided against the FBI on the grounds of illegal search, and upholding citizens' rights to privacy and secretive conversations. Update: The USA Patriots Act permits government certain widespread monitoring of communications technologies, and ex-intelligence worker Snowden's media exposure of the extent of "government spying" has created public backlash against the NSA and government snooping.

Conclusion and Opinion: The Ultimate Secret Is Out There

Ponce de Leon searched for the "Fountain of Youth" and ended up discovering the Pacific Ocean and Native Americans. His quest, however continues to this day at an accelerated pace. Today's cosmetic surgical techniques will give way to stem cell "stews", cloning of organs and complete "brainless" bodies, xeno-transplantations, cerebral transplantation, and spinal cord regeneration that will make it possible for the wealthy who can afford it to attain not only the appearance of youth, but generational life extension, perhaps perpetual youth and immortality.

The proliferation of technological secrets, and the attempts to use technology to protect secrets that contain quantum leaps in scientific and technological advances with profound social, economic, political, and military implications is necessarily justified. The consequences from the disclosure of secrets could have serious negative potential on a national, global, and species level. Individuals, governments, corporations, and the military all attempt to tightly guard their secrets, but technology and highly educated individuals make safeguarding secrets problematic.

With the rapid dawning of a new age of computers, biotechnology, genomics, and new self-replicating nano-materials, trade and military secrets are subject to heightened assaults from both internal and external sources; from employees, ex-officials, spies, competitors, and enemies.

Secrecy is the oil that lubricates the wheels of society, because most human beings don't appear capable of accepting any truth that is contrary to their mental and emotional prejudices. After all, humans have created religion, culture, and superstition to assuage their inner most fears of the unknown and unpredictable. As scientific discoveries and its technological applications become more common place, and revolutionizes the manner in which human beings relate to each other in societies and civilizations, there will be periods of discontinuity, and dangerous unforeseeable consequences of new knowledge. While the potential promise of bringing greater control over the environment appears within mankind's grasp, humanity's tendency to be myopic, egocentric, curious, and selfishly blind makes the species vulnerable to setbacks on a potential extinction level.

Perhaps all knowledge may not be good to know. Perhaps we've taken too many steps to embrace forbidden knowledge, which instead of bringing us further liberation, will instead enslave or destroy us. Have we already passed the point of no return? Long before we may be able to breed our perfect clones, or create human-animal-plant-crustacean interspecies hybrids capable of interplanetary colonization, terrorists will be able to secretly use Internet anonymity to explode briefcase sized nukes aboard commercial jets landing at large metropolitan airports, or aboard cargo containers sitting offshore on ships at busy ports of call. And while mankind attempts to replace nature as the creator of all life, we may unwittingly create a way for new life forms to replace mankind. The margin of life as we know it on earth occupies a relatively narrow window. We don't know what the outcomes will be when our scientific curiosity and technological greed accidentally crosses our species over and beyond our window of existence in the universe. And that, Sherlock, is why we need secrecy. Nature's secrets should remain secret, as mankind has shown himself to be the boy who plays with fire, then burns everything down around him. Technology is not the panacea for mankind's problems, but rather it may become the curse.

The Global Power Paradigm

It is obvious that the greatest powers in the world from Alexander the Great, the Romans, the Spanish, English, Germans, Russians and Americans have represented nations with homogeneous ethnic white majorities. It has also been the American and European capitalistic investments in cheap labor and materials from Third World Nations that has resulted in their economic developing in the past 40 years, with China rapidly becoming an economic power only in the past two decades. Global power economic and military power remains in the hands of white majoritarian nations.

Since the end of WW2, Americans have witnessed tumultuous times amidst astounding scientific and technological advances, for better and for worse. They have witnessed via the media and Internet, volumes of photographs, videos, and reports of human atrocities against humans. Americans were spared home front battlefields during WW2, but the decades of violence that followed were in many ways equally abhorrent as more American residents and citizens have died from violence than were killed in all of our wars. The civil rights era, the Vietnam War, assassinations of JFK, MLK, RFK, Malcolm X, Gandhi, and many lesser known patriots and humanitarians set the stage for contemporary state and non-state acts of violence.

The horrific inhumanity of the Jewish Holocaust of 6 million people was only a few decades later followed by Pol Pot's Khmer Rouge slaughter of perhaps upwards of 8 million Cambodians. Idi Amin was known to laugh out loud when slaughtering hundreds of thousands of his own people in Uganda, the Tutus and Hutus still kill each other in Rwandans, as China had witnessed the executions, imprisonment, and torture of millions. It has not been a peaceful world, as technology has both advanced the efficiency and effectiveness of violence, while acting as a partial deterrent in the international arena.

People have wondered silently why these atrocities were allowed to continue over the years by the Western political/military elites, who typically foster grand sounding humanitarian ideals, yet whose actions have often proven to betray those principles they pretend to espouse. Isn't the life of an African, or Asian, or Jew equally worth that of a Briton, American, German, or Swede? I surmise from standard of living statistics, that in the scales of the First World Hegemony, the answer was an emphatic "NO." Therein lies the basis of the international struggle between peoples, races, and ethnic groups. American history provides a prime example of First World tactics, when the genocide of Native Americans followed a pattern of false promises, broken treaties, and military violence that had become the international standard.

What does the First World Hegemony want that entails tolerance of inhumanity in non-white states and support of oppressive juntas in third world nations, which it attempts to prevent in Europe? I'm convinced that the historical colonialist mentality still runs strongly through the blood lines of Europe's elites; only the revisionist strategy for world domination no longer lies in direct military confrontation, but in global economic control and domination, juxtaposed by military intimidation. Their vision continues to be one of a united Europe as the center of civilization, a feat first attempted by European royalty, and now made possible by the creation of multi-national corporate conglomerates owned by Europe's elites. What they weren't able to accomplish with real people, they now are accomplishing through fictional entities (legal immortal corporations) and the utilization of technology.

Europe is in fact no more than a fictional continent created to satisfy an egomaniacal self-aggrandizing overcompensating need for their early backward and warring heritages. Europe is not physically a continent, but merely the western end of the Asian continent. This drive to create fictional entities (corporations), fictional (and worthless) monetary systems, deceptive and untruthful marketing, political, and bureaucratic institutions and ideals are all part of their larger scheme of world domination. The First World Anglo-Germanic European-American plan for world domination is essentially the same in principle as it was when "The sun never set on the British Empire", only the methods have been disguised and repackaged to appear beneficial to the peace and economic development of the developing world. It's a sales pitch that is leading the Third World eventually to genocide.

The smoke screen for the new world order is the accelerating dependency of developing world markets on the Western monetary system, the creation of a future justification for military intervention to protect Western assets, and the future wholesale rape of third world resources as repayment to World Bank members. The gradual genocide of Third World peoples through poverty, disease, racism, class warfare, violence, and military interventions (conventional, genetic, and nuclear) are the future methods of genocide. At the rate AIDS is decimating the population in Sub-Saharan Africa, NATO and UN troops, backed by First World corporate interests, will be called on in the future to "stabilize" Africa's infrastructure, as a pretext to develop its vast stores of natural resources for western products and consumption. Bulldozers and the tracks of military vehicles will carve the "silk road" to the eventual rape of Africa. A neo-Socratic examination of Waltz's arguable notions comparing structure in the highly centralized hierarchic domestic state versus the decentralized anarchic international environmental context of the realism paradigm. In the case of international relations, Waltz opined that state interactions, human relations, and functional differences within and between states has no real consequences, that the only factors of importance is the structural positioning of states as units that compete for survival through self-help self-propagation activities in competition with other states to determine who has the greatest degree of power (military-economic). It is the structure or positioning of power that stimulates the games states feel compelled to play to protect themselves against current and potential enemies, which determines consequences in the anarchic global disorder.

The issue of social contract per Hobbs, and how the state uses police force to intimidate its citizens to comply with its laws was discussed. Not mentioned in class was that Rousseau viewed *Social Contract* as a way to alleviate, among other things, the main cause of our evils (Scott, 1992: 708). Rousseau felt that morals seem to be of two types: that which is moral in being "established" by "a sort of convention" as men begin to associate together, and a "political" form that is moral in the sense of being "authorized" by the consent of man as a social contract. Rousseau felt that humans exist purely as physical beings, possessed solely of physical instincts, passions, and faculties; and man originally lacked moral needs or passions, or conscious regards for their fellow humans (Scott, 1992: 702). Waltz views states purely as physical structures, possessed solely of the instinct of self-preservation corresponding to their power position in an anarchistic world, without regards to moral needs, passions, or conscious regards for humanity.

Few politicians or academicians will publicly admit or profess to discern the reality that stares down humanity today, and the likely outcomes of global political-economic policies dictated by the First World bloc of nations that comprises the white race. Their methods of self-propagation are many, including technological advantage, genetic weapons, economic destabilization, cultural imperialism, and first strike nuclear projection. Is it their goal to eventually limit world population to 2 billion humans, comprised of 1 billion whites (Alphas), and 1 billion colored races (Betas). Is their hidden agenda to rid the world of the poor, illiterate, disabled, retarded, and non-elites over 50 that comprises over 80 percent of the planet's colored races?

Applying a global market economy paradigm, the Betas would serve the Alphas by producing goods and services from industries owned by the Alphas. Based upon Marxist theory, the Alphas would own the means of production, and the Betas would supply the labor. The Alphas (bourgeoisie) would obtain the best, with the lesser grade products available to the Betas (workers class). This "ideal" configuration will save the planetary environment by eliminating pollution from developing nations, massive waste products of human consumption, and the depletion of natural resources by an exploding world population (projected to reach 30 billion by 2100, if supportable by earth). The world would become relatively stable because the white hegemony of so-called democratic states will be able to manage world resources according to the WTO & World Bank "standards." Developing nations, weakened by AIDS and diseases from GM (genetically modified) foods, will depend on the West to assist them, which will instead present a Trojan horse, the appearance of benign humanitarian aid, laced with genetic disease, political corruption, and economic dependency.

The First World Hegemony's Anti-Third-World Genocidal Strategy is expressed as economic dominance by the IMF and World Bank; dependency of developing nations' economies under the threat of monetary destabilization. The west is waiting for AIDS to decimate and weaken African and Asian governments to the point they may step in to "restore order and for humanitarian reasons", install corrupt puppet governments, and then export the natural resources of those continents while enslaving their peoples to supply cheap labor for products of western consumption.

The current global power paradigm involves several layers of control, including cultural imperialism via the Internet, music, movies, clothing, food, and other deceptive marketing ploys to "sanitize" the world of non-western ideas, customs, cultures, and religions that do not conform to the ideal profit making motive of the global market system; political colonialism via infectious spread of "scientific management" and other western legal and bureaucratic concepts, and through bribery and corruption of developing world governmental elites and utilization of food and medicines as coercive strategies. In addition, military domination by embargo of developing nuclear states, supporting destabilization of non-cooperative states, projecting secret genetic and viral warfare materials into the Third World (e.g., AIDS, genetically modified foods), developing a nuclear missile shield, and targeting nukes at developing Third World nations as future nuclear extortion are essential strategies to supporting the status quo power paradigm.

Global capitulation to the First World Hegemony from intrinsic threats of complete annihilation and devastation from secret weapons demonstrates potential hegemonic swaggering. Black genocide is a systemic, historical and contemporary attack on and degradation, reduction, and eventual elimination of the black race. The United States of America Hegemony espouses high democratic and humanitarian ideals, and the majority of its peoples wear Christian values on their sleeves and many demonstrate compassion and charity. However, on closer examination, there lies an undercurrent of hatred, racism and class division that tears at the fabric of American ideas. What part does America play as an initiator, supporter, and implementer of regime change that often leads to instability and genocide?

The ABM system and the projection of First World nuclear and economic power against the Third World are parts of a secretly formulated strategy to give world dominance and control to Euro-America. History and contemporary events indicate that there exist a real (secret), though subtle conspiracy among the Anglo-Germanic elites (and their white American descendants) who control world resources to maintain their superior position through policies that directly or indirectly result in the genocide of the world's non-whites.

REFERENCES for *The Cost Benefits of Secrecy:*

Adams, James. The Next World War. Computers Are the Weapons and the Front Line Is Everywhere. New York, NY: Simon & Schuster, 1998.

Anton, Philip W., Richard Silberglitt & James Schneider. "Biotechnology, Nano-Materials Trends and Their Synergies with Information Technology by 2015" *The Global Technology Revolution.* Santa Monica, CA: RAND, 2001. Retrieved May 13, 2001 from the Internet: http://www.rand.org

Denning, Dorothy E. and Herbert S. Lin., Editors. Right and esponsibilities of Participants in Networked Communities. Washington D.C.: National Academy Press, 1994.

Diamond v.Chakrabarty. Retrieved May 19, 2001 from the Internet: http://oyez.at.nwu.edu/cases/cases.cgi?case_id=1125&command=show

Ez Detective. Retrieved May 6, 2001 from the World Wide Web: http://www.ezdetective.com/index3.html

Friedman, Robert I. Red Mafiya. How the Russian Mob Has Invaded America. New York, NY: Little, Brown and Company, 2000.

Huerta, Tim. Retrieved May 19, 2001 from the World Wide Web: **http://www-scf.usc.edu/~thuerta/POLS579**

Katz v. United States. Retrieved May 19, 2001 from the World Wide Web: http://oyez.at.nwu.edu/cases/cases.cgi?case_id=198&command=show

Lesser, I & B. Hoffman, et. al. "MR-989-AF, Countering the New Terrorism." Retrieved May 12, 2001 from the Internet: **http://www.rand.org/paf/highlights/terrorism3.html**

Macintyre, Ben. The Napoleon of Crime The Life and Times of Adam Worth, Master Thief. New York, NY: Farrar, Straus and Giroux, 1997.

Mark, P.J. "What Is 'IT'?" *Inside.* (January 9, 2001). Retrieved from http://www.inside.com/jcs/Story?article_id=20218&pod_id=8

Milken. Milken Institute. Retrieved May 11, 2001 from the World Wide Web: http://www.milkeninstitute.org/mod35/mir4_48_inflation.pdf

NES. National Election Study, 1996 data set. Retrieved May 12, 2001 from the World Wide Web: http://csa.berkeley.edu

Persinger, M.A. "Possibility of Direct Access to Every Human Brain." *Rumor Mill News Forum.* Laurentian University, 1995. Retrieved May 7, 2001 from the World Wide Web: **http://www.rumormillnews.com/cgi-bin/config.pl?read=2929**

Puharich. "New Frontiers Center Newsletter," Spring-Summer 1984, Nos. 9 & 10. pages 5-6. Retrieved May 6, 2001 from the World Wide Web: http://www.geocities.com/Area51/Shadowlands/6583/secret.html

RAND. "The Paradox of the Secrecy About Secrecy" Retrieved May 12, 2001 from the Internet: http://www.rand.org/publications/RM/RM3765/RM3765.chapter2.html

Shawdowlands. "Area 51" Retrieved May 6, 2001 from the World Wide Web: http://www.geocities.com/Area51/Shadowlands

Woodward Jr., John D. "And Now, the Good Side of Facial Profiling." *Washington Post.* February 4, 2001. Retrieved May 11, 2001 from the World Wide Web: **http://www.rand.org/hot/op-eds/020401WP.html**

References for *The Global Power Paradigm:*

Jonathan Benthall. "Fox Among the Lambs." *Anthropology Today*, Vol. 5, No. 3. (Jun., 1989), pp. 1-2.

Kyle Grimes. "The Entropics of Discourse: Michael Harper's Debridement and the Myth of the Hero." *Black American Literature Forum*, Vol. 24, No. 3. (Autumn, 1990), pp. 417-440.

Christopher Keith Hall. "The First Five Sessions of the UN Preparatory Commission for the International Criminal Court (in Current Developments)."*American Journal of International Law*, Vol. 94, No. 4. (Oct., 2000), pp. 773-789.

LaRouche, Jr., Lyndon H. "Now, Are You Ready To Learn Economics? Washington D.C.: EIR News Service, Inc., 2000.

LaRouche, Jr., Lyndon H. "The Road To Recovery" Leesburg, VA: New Bretton Woods, 1999. Socialist Worker Number 370 (June 8, 2001), pg.

Liisa H. Malkki. "Refugees and Exile: From "Refugee Studies" to the National Order of Things." *Annual Review of Anthropology*, Vol. 24. (1995), pp. 495-523.

Carole Nagengast. "Violence, Terror, and the Crisis of the State."*Annual Review of Anthropology*, Vol. 23. (1994), pp. 109-136.

Neuhouser, Frederick. "Freedom, Dependency, and the General Will." *The Philosophical Review*, Volume 102, Issue 3 (Jul. 1993), pg. 363-395.

Scott, John T. "The Theodicy of the Second Discourse: The 'Pure State of Nature' and Rousseau's Political Thought." *The American Political Science Review*, Volume 86, Issue 3 (Sep. 1992), pgs. 696-711.

Debora Shuger. "Irishmen, Aristocrats, and Other White Barbarians" *Renaissance Quarterly*, Vol. 50, No. 2. (Summer, 1997), pp. 494-525.
M. Estellie Smith. "The Process of Sociocultural Continuity. "*Current Anthropology*, Vol. 23, No. 2. (Apr., 1982), pp. 127-142.

THE EVOLUTION OF MANKIND INTO A RACE OF KILLERS

Modern humans are supposedly more enlightened than those of previous eras where the vast armies of emperors and kings attacked, killed, raped and plundered other peoples and cultures to expand their personal empires. But are modern humans in fact a more peaceful race? If we look at the statistics, the warfare paradigm hasn't changed since the time of Alexander the Great as imperialism, colonialism, revolution, regime change and false flag wars continue to take the lives of millions.

The history of the evolution of mankind from tribes to nation-states has been strewed with violence, murder, rape, plundering, torture and great inhumanities.

1.   The earliest traces of *homo-sapiens*, humans, as we know the species today was in Africa, approximately 4 million years ago, and while other hominid, perhaps as many as a dozen races have appeared on planet earth, none has survived to this day, besides *homo-sapiens*.

2.   Approximately 200 families from the African human gene pool migrated to what is now modern day Europe. Why, we can only surmise. Perhaps a nomadic tribe of hunter-gatherers (as there were no farmers in those times) wandered for generations before settling in Europe.

3.   The weather and eco-system in ancient Europe was probably not as cold as it is nowadays, but as the continents continued to drift apart, that portion, which is now called Europe, continued to drift northward, and closer to the north pole, an increasingly colder region.

4.   Over a time span of hundreds of thousands, and perhaps a million years, the descendants of the original 200 families evolved in adaptation to the climate, an eco-system that was not lush as was mother Africa, with fewer wild beasts and animals, less vegetation and fruits, and snow many months of the year. Those who became most adaptive to the colder climates, survived, and produced progeny. Those who didn't, died .

5.   Some of the requisite genetic adaptations would have been, a lightening of the skin color, for hunting camouflage advantages, eventually blending in with the white snow. Other beneficial survival predispositions would have been emotional traits, such as aggressiveness, jealousy, greed, fear, distrust, possessiveness, materialism, curiosity, exploration, power lust, and love.

6.   Aggressiveness to follow and chase down sparse populations of animals needed for food. Jealousy required bonding and settling down with females to provide a family environment for procreating and protecting the family unit essential for future generations. Greed gave the added motivation to hoard food to last through icy cold winters (free refrigeration). Fear and distrust kept survivors from succumbing to competitive or predatory stranger families, tribes and animals. Possessiveness drove men to claim and protect territories, to ensure survival food and shelter resources. Materialism causes humans to become inventive, as they sought to create and own things of beauty and comfort for themselves. Curiosity and exploration drove men to conquer new territories. Power lust led men to conquer others, to feel superior to others, and love for family, friends, and tribe justified the use of power to conquer others.

7.   As the descendants of the original 200 families evolved into the white race, they inherited and taught various survival skills and cultural ideas to seceding generations, with the positive result of species survival and growth. As the population grew and social interactions evolved to as a result of language, and civilizations ensued. City-states, kingdoms, and eventually nation-states become formalized sovereign structures that enhanced the development of hierarchical political structures and organizations, permitting military conquest and imperialism.

8.   The rest of the world lived in tropical environments, Africa, Asia, and later the new world, the Americas. The inhabitants of tropical and semi-tropical environments enjoyed the abundance of animal and plant life, ample for natural survival. The greater natural abundance in

Africa and the Americas in general reduced the need for tribal conflicts, however a handful of civilizations arose that attempted to unite territorial tribes to conquer smaller neighboring groups. In Asia, philosophical and cultural traditions enabled relatively stable civilizations to flourish amidst a bounty of natural resources.

9.   As the rest of the world produced sufficient food and resources to sustain its inhabitants, Europeans were embroiled in constant inter-regional conflicts that persisted to contemporary times. Military interventions were the operative strategy to obtain resources that they lacked, leading to imperialism, colonialism, and world wars. The white race's heightened aggressiveness, distrust, greed, and other inherited predispositions justified and enhanced their ability to subjugate of less hostile races, who were less equipped technologically and militarily to resist the white race's expansionism. While early Chinese civilization invented and use black powder for celebratory fireworks and rockets, the white races perfected its use as gunpowder, bombs and propellant for canon balls.

10.   The white race became the world's pre-eminent purveyors of death and destruction, and in the rare cases where they were not the direct implementers of violence, they created economic inequities, political, and societal environments in other cultures and countries where genocide resulted through the actions of deranged military-political juntas, often the puppet governments installed by white colonizer nations, such as Idi Amin in Uganda and Pol Pot in Cambodia. The white race's obsession with improving the methods and technology of mass destruction and death led to the development of the widely used chemical and biological weapons of WWI, nuclear bombs of WW2, and ICBMs of the Cold War. The inventiveness of the white race has made them into the First World of nations, giving them economic and military advantage and dominance over the rest of the world, comprised primarily of colored-people, now numbering 5 billion people, or 5/6ths of the human population.

11.   The new weapons of mass destruction that probably have already been developed include the neutron bomb, viruses more deadly and persistent than Anthrax, genetically targeting ethnic genocidal weapons transferable through perspiration or saliva, airborne particulates, or via genetically modified foods and drinks, or via insects or nano-materials. Will WW3 be the long-awaited "race war" that is a fundamental tenet of white supremacists groups; however, not fought by bullets between the races in urban and rural enclaves, but instead by a slow, insidious, and undetectable decrease of life span of non-whites through new genocidal weapons? Certainly the great disparity between the life styles enjoyed by the average of white inhabitants of planet earth, by far, surpass that of 90 percent of the world's colored peoples, half of whom barely live subsistence lives, and fully more than one-third living in destitute with persistent hunger and disease. As the white race's global colonization and economic exploitation has been the primary factors that created the imbalance and heightened disparity between the "haves" (the white race), and the "have nots" (the colored races, except for a minority of non-white elites who are dependent and in collusion with white elites), the suffering of humanity can be traced directly to political, economic, and military exploitation by First World nations.

12.   What are the likely outcomes of the continuation of genocidal policies by the First World? Is there a secret plan to promote the survival of the white race over that of non-whites? What are the conditions that will be necessary to legitimize the genocidal policies of the First World hegemony to permit a more open declaration and quickening of the white elite's plan for global domination, the pre-eminence of the white race as global rulers, and the subservience of non-whites as the servants of whites (until their labor can be totally replaced by computers, robots, and genetically engineered transpecies hybrids) who are not a threat to their white rulers?

13.   In order to propose hypothetical answers to the above questions, based on historical facts and precedents, let's consider the following facts:

a. The white race has essentially wiped out the red race within 500 years.

b. The white race enslaved the black race for over 400 hundred years, and continue to institutionalize socio-economic conditions that subjugates the majority of the world's black people to poverty and violence.

c. The white race colonized almost all of Asia, or forced it into unequal trade relationships for almost one hundred years.

d. The white race is willing to kill its own white people on a massive basis, such as WWI and WW2, and to cause genocide such was done to the Jews during WW2.

e. There are approximately 1 billion white people in the world, compared to over 6 billion non-white people, of whom almost 4.5 billion are of the yellow race (East Indians and Chinese are genetic relatives), and 1.5 billion are of the black or brown races (including Middle-Easterners). It is highly doubtful planet earth can support more than 30 billion people, a population that arithmetically could be reached within this century. The planet would strain to feed even half that projected number based on the dismal failure of humanitarian support of at least 3 billion of the world's current inhabitants, over 90% who are non-white. The environmental pollution from the developing world engorged by sustained population explosion would be staggering.

f. Inherited similarities exist among racial and ethnic groups, and actual differences between individuals far exceed that between the races.

g. HIV-AIDS attack less than 1% of the white population, while its infective rate is alarming among the non-white populations of Africa, Asia, Latin-America, and even among colored people who reside in the First World. Sub-Saharan Africa has an AIDs infection rate exceeding half of its population, with no cure in sight. Was AIDs actually a genetically engineered viral weapon of genocide spread to Africans during the 1970s as part of an unwitting UN smallpox inoculation program, or the result of one monkey bite? The math discounts the monkey bite as the cause of the AIDS epidemic. More likely, the introduction of AIDS to over 2 million Africans via a genocidal weapon, disguised as a humanitarian program, a Trojan Horse.

h. More than 80% of Asians are lactose intolerant, a fact borne out from observing that most yellow skinned peoples are allergic to cow's milk.

i. A markedly higher percentage of Americans of the black race inherit the genes that make them susceptible to sickle cell anemia, as compared to whites.

j. Technologist develop chemicals that attract and cling to cockroaches, that do not kill them for several days, permitting them to "infect" other roaches, a genocidal strategy.

k. Technologist genetically modify plants to secret chemicals that are toxic to insects, fungi, and other competitive or predatory plants, more genocidal strategies.

l. Over 2/3rds of known species of plants, animals, insects, fishes, birds, snakes, and other life have become extinct in the past 100 years... massive genocide.

m. By perfecting genetic engineering and cloning technology, extinct or endanger species may someday be brought back, and new transpecies life forms developed.

n. Cloning humans may have already been accomplished several decades ago, but will certainly be accomplished within the next decade.

o. Stem cells and cloning technologies, once perfected, may enable the wealthy and global elites (95% of whom are white) to live for over a thousand year (studies indicate that short of injury or disease, the brain is constantly replenishing its cellular mass,

and continues to make new neuron connections and new synaptic pathways, or perhaps to attain immortality. This may be possible with the next 20 years.

p. If a man can will pay 20 million dollars for a ride to outer space, how much would genetic rejuvenation and possible immortality be worth? Priceless.

14. How can the world's colored peoples fight against genocide? Do they stand "a Chinaman's chance"? If the world's 1.5 billion Chinese (including Taiwan, overseas Chinese, Chinese descendants in Pacific Rim), with the 2nd largest economy in the world, after the United States, with over 500 nuclear weapons, with sophisticated scientific and technological capabilities, can't save themselves from the genocidal scenarios of event horizon, then who can? Perhaps, like the Japanese, the Chinese will surrender to the white race hegemony, and capitulate themselves to a supporting role, with the white race as the Alphas, and the yellow race as the Betas. The book by Aldous Huxley, "Brave New World" described the future racial and class configuration of global society, where the dark-skinned races will be relegated to menial labor.

15. Already, the consistent trend is for one-third of Asian females who reside in the First World to intermarry and produced mixed-race offsprings, over two-thirds of whom marry whites. On the other hand, less than 5% of Asian males residing in the First World marry white women,

more often for race-based preferences of white women, who generally do not find Asian men to be sexually appealing. At any rate, the white male is accustomed to conquering non-white peoples, then fucking the conquered people's women; however, they protest and become enraged when colored peoples (like the black slaves of the deep south, or poor blacks of the north) fuck "their" white women. Consequently, many socially or economically successful non-Whites feel they have a higher sense of social and thus self-respect when they can fuck white.

16.   The racial phenotype outcome of racially mixed genotype is generally non-white, consequently, if more whites mix breed their progeny, and this is carried on and gains acceptance generation after generation, the extrapolated, however unlikely result will be the extinction of the white race (a sworn belief of the KKK, neo-Nazis, white supremacists, and Aryan militias). Long before the white race will become extinct through interracial mixing, the white elites will launch genocidal weapons of mass destruction against non-white races. Why? Because they have the technology, economic and military power to keep non-whites in check by killing them, or having their non-white surrogates perform genocide is a simple historical fact.

17.   Could the white race function at their higher standards of living, without the exploitation of non-whites? Robots have replaced many higher paid industrial workers, the majority who have been white, but it is still cheaper to hire low wage non-white workers in the developing world than to develop and use robots in most parts of assembly or manufacturing. As robotics technology becomes more miniaturized, more sophisticated in applications, more mobile, user-friendly, and cheaper to mass produce and purchase, the white race will reorganize its global economic paradigm to ensure lives of comfort for white inhabitants, and total disregard for non-whites laborers.

Are most whites willing to do the menial, repetitious, low-skilled, and low-pay jobs that under-educated non-whites are forced by poverty to accept? How often do we see whites serving non-whites in low-paying service jobs traditionally assigned to colored people, like farm worker, maid, and janitor? And while many teenagers at one time work in the fast food industry, across racial, ethnic, and gender lines, the hierarchical stratification of the employment market reflect a more master-servant relationship between white CEOs, administrators, and managers and their non-white subordinates in career path positions, especially lucrative ones.

19.   Within a decade, grocery and fast food purchases will be commonly made by speech recognition computers that operate automatic assembly lines fed by robotic arms that will scan items and deduct costs from credit/debit cards. In less than 50 years, robots will be able to replace humans in performing most tasks, from the most menial to the most complex. Unemployment will be the most serious societal problem, followed by hunger, shelter, disease, mental illness, and violence. The genetically modified white super race will no longer need to exploit impoverished colored races to do things they can have robots do more efficiently, without complaints or threats.

20. Once the elite white super race no longer needs non-white people, except for entertainment or other non-essential activities, the secret genetic ethnic genocidal weapons will be unleashed. The methods of transmission will be many, including insects, nano-molecules, water, food, medicine, alcohol, and other environmental circumstances most common among Third World populations and non-white neighborhoods in the First World, like New York City, Chicago and Los Angeles. We appear to be living on the "Planet of the Apes" here on Earth, where gorillas, chimpanzees, and baboons act more "humanely" to other members of their own species, than human beings generally act to each other. And while

First World nations seemingly are champions of human rights and animal rights (their pet cats and dogs), their record of global economic and political policies reinforce a dichotomous environment of more for the rich, and less for the poor.

One major deterrent to overt genocide is the world banking community, greatly influenced by Jews, because they have not forgotten their Holocaust in WW2 Europe. Large productive populations still factor into the global economic equation as sources of cheap labor and mass consumption, which maximizes profits for the global elites and bankers. However, as the cost of labor eventually increases past the point of optimal profits, a new balance will be struck between profit potential versus cost of production and consumer purchasing power. They will decide that a world of 2 billion consumers paying top dollar for products manufactured by robots will be preferable to 7 billion consumers paying paltry dollars for products manufactured by low paid workers. Then perhaps genocide will become more overt, justified by environmental concerns as a strategy to arrest pollution, exhaustion of natural resources, and planetary decay.

One major deterrent to overt genocide is the world banking community, greatly influenced by Jews, because they have not forgotten their Holocaust in WW2 Europe. Large productive populations still factor into the global economic equation as sources of cheap labor and mass consumption, which maximizes profits for the global elites and bankers. However, as the cost of labor eventually increases past the point of optimal profits, a new balance will be struck between profit potential versus cost of production and consumer purchasing power. They will decide that a world of 2 billion consumers paying top dollar for products manufactured by robots will be preferable to 7 billion consumers paying paltry dollars for products manufactured by low paid workers. Then perhaps genocide will become more overt, justified by environmental concerns as a strategy to arrest pollution, exhaustion of natural resources, and planetary decay.

As this scenario unfolds, many ethical, moral, and humanitarian white individuals will protest and "fight" for colored people's right to life. The result will be menial compromises to increase the number of non-whites who will be allowed a chance to live, subject to strict criteria to permit only the top colored gene pools to survive. Genetic engineering of surviving non-whites will make them obedient, subservient, and non-threatening to whites. Crimes against white people by non-whites will automatically carry the death sentence. For all this effort, the non-white population will be allowed to increase by 10 million people, or 1 percent, to justify increasing the white population by 2 percent, in accordance to the formula, "two new white lives for every colored life", a caste system of master-to-servant. Poverty, disease, and joblessness for colored peoples will be eliminated because the poor, disabled, and elderly non-whites will be euthanized. The First World's program to exterminate third world peoples as part of Malthusian population control efforts of the new world order secret government.

Conclusion:

The racist paradigm of the old world order elitist-controlled entertainment industry, that the new world order is the same old world order, only a more efficient model that the greedy ignorant masses have bought into as productive global marketization that benefits the poor and developing nations, when in fact it just creates greater dependency of the masses and third world peoples on the corrupt and bankrupt international monetary system, that racist and selective population control measures are even now being perfected as we collectively sleep, that will be unleashed upon the world when the secret world government feels the time is right (in the combination of neutron bombs, genetic/viral warfare, and ELFs -extra low frequency weapons that can alter weather, cause massive earthquakes and volcanoes, and alter or debilitate human brain waves on large regional levels). Mass media and the movie and music industry already use such ELF technology in creating and manipulating the emotional mood of its audiences, as ELFs are subharmonic, and can't be heard. an example of this technology are "sub-woofers" that causes your body to vibrate, yet can't be heard, only ELFs are far more advanced and dangerous.

Faced against these circumstances, how can a person not become cynical? unless people who are loyal to the secret world government, who control the weapons of mass destruction, refuse to cooperate with their masters (but like the air traffic controllers of the Reagan era, they can all be fired and replaced by others), the masses will remain essentially impotent in the face of what has described as the impending total economic collapse of the global market and financial system. While this collapse will be catastrophic against the world's middle class, it will have a beneficial effect for the world's elites, bleeding the last vestiges of capital wealth from the middle class, and to restore the world to the original dichotomous world power paradigm of the ruling class owning the land, resources and government along with the people who are their subjects, slaves, serfs, servants that comprise the poor class.

All governments that currently cooperate in playing the globalization game are lining their own pockets, while their national populations benefit relatively in small increments (except the corrupt and criminal always make great strides) as reward for their capitulation and keeping the masses under control, these government leaders in the third and second worlds will be rewarded and shielded against economic harm when the world's economic system collapses for the masses. When everything has collapsed, all the stock values can be bought back at basement prices, and the elites shall devise a new set of relationships among themselves for dividing up the spoils of Africa, Asia, and Latin America. Surely there will be mass rioting and civil unrest, but all that does is pit the masses against themselves, as ethnic and racial groups will primarily attack each other. National and global militaries will be called upon to quell the violence with lethal force, and tens of millions of political and religious activists will be arrested and caged in concentration camps. Later, as mass violence gets "out of control", the military will resort to the use of neutron bombs, genetic/viral weapons, and ELFs sent from orbiting satellites to subdue the masses. It will be a carnage never witnessed before on the face of the earth, as billions of people will be annihilated.

The reptilian Satanic secret world order will have its revenge for the destruction of its reptilian ancestors, the dinosaurs who were at least twice subjected to mass extinction, then survived and parts of its genetic code mixed with mammalian DNA, then eventually evolved into certain lineages of homo sapiens, who became the aggressive leaders and the elites of the modern day world. Sounds far out and some people think these ideas sound crazy, but ideas that exposes the truth about the corruption of the status quo have always been labeled as crazy, to discredit their new ideas and insights with the masses as a strategy to discourage rebellion. The system is not afraid of individuals because 99% of people would probably think the reptilian notion is sci-fi and ridiculous, but a simple comparison of human and lizard DNA shows similarities, and as the human embryo goes through its stages of development, at one point, it resembles reptilian form.

Mankind was seeded on this planet from outer space, whether God or another more advanced civilization like the Annunaki from Nibiru or maybe from Mars, then combined with that life which was on earth (primarily reptilian), before evolving to human beings. Many human beings have long and pointed reptilian tongues and reptilian looking eyes? Geneticists call it genetic defects, or whatever, but in fact those are recessive genes left from the reptilian super species that once roamed and ruled the earth, descendants of the great dinosaurs who roamed ancient Earth for around 165 million years, and whose descendants now rule Earth as the secret world government. Many people would find these alien ideas to be weird, but weird only means unusual, and not untruthful or disproved. Just because something has not been "proven" by science (maybe they don't have the right type of technology or aren't looking in the right places), doesn't mean it's been disproved. In fact, the bulk of discovery has been the eventual proof of previously unproven or ridiculous notions and theories that have been viewed as dangerous to the status quo.

The God Paradigm

Are Reptilian-Human hybrids from Satan? The Bible and scientists are in agreement about the outcomes of events that were described in the Bible, however scientific arrogance do not describe the events as evidence of Biblical proportions. Case in point. According to the Bible, God cast Lucifer, or Satan, out of Heaven along with one-third of the angels who rose up in defiance of Jehovah Almighty Creator God. Satan had taken the form of a serpent to entice Eve, who enticed Adam, the original human beings, to sin, and who were also subsequently cast out of heaven. When the Bible was written, humans did not have the technology of space travel, or the deep space Hubble Telescope, or biotechnology-genetics knowledge. Their interpretations of Biblical events were both figurative and symbolic. Now, we see that scientific facts actually support the description of Biblical events.

Take for instance Creation Theory vs. the Big Bang and Evolution theories. God created the universe from nothing. Isn't that basically what the Big Bang theory states? That all of the matter in the universe came from super dense "black matter" which exploded to form the stars, planets, and all the mass in the known universe? And Satan, the serpent (a lizard), was cast on to the planet earth, from Heaven. These serpentine creatures became the dinosaurs that lived for around 165 million years before the first humans arrived on the scene. And Satan was given rulership over the earth, and its inhabitants. And hasn't mankind been evil during most of his recorded history? Violence, killing, and wars became mankind's calling. An asteroid wiped out over 85% of dinosaurs and life on earth during the Triassic Period, which ushered in the Jurassic Period, almost 200 million years ago. About 56 million years ago, another meteor, comet, or asteroid wiped out over 95% of all life on earth, in the seas and on land. Could it be that very small dinosaurs survived here and there, in caves, or borough underground, that evolved into modern day lizards and snakes? And could it be possible that some of the genes from lizards mixed with mammalian genes when the earth had reverted to a melting pot genetic soup after the cataclysmic near-extinction meteor strike. And could it be that certain forms of bacteria was able to link certain amino acid and protein strains between lizard and hominid early on, during the stem cells reproduction stage of development?

As mankind evolved from intentional hybridization (God's method of creation), from a mixture of gene pool between lizard and ape into the original homo-sapiens hominid in Africa over 4 million years ago, the gene for evil and violence passed from Satan into mankind genetic code. As time evolved, some of Satan's lineage became rulers of man, as God had given Satan dominion over the earth. That is one reason most earthly governments have persecuted and exploited mankind to build riches for the elites who rule the world. God also said that we can not worship two masters; either we worship God through expressing love for our fellow humans, or we worship Satan, by seeking to acquire money and materialism, often through force, deception, manipulation, and excessive profits that has typified the unequal trading position between the rich and powerful, versus the poor and humble. God also said that "the meek" shall inherit the earth, not the rich and powerful that owns 90% of the world's resources today, with the top 1% owning 75% of the world.

God also warned that in the end times, we should see evidence in the heavens of things never before witnessed by man. The Hubble Telescope showed us two galaxies colliding, and many wonders beyond our wildest imaginations. Mankind witnessed for the first time, a meteor break up as it struck Jupiter, any one fragment causing explosions on Jupiter larger than the entire size of the Earth. Revelations describes several meteors falling from the heavens, one of which scorched one-third of the earth, killing one-third of its inhabitants, and another name "wormwood" that cause half of the rivers and oceans to turn poisonous and reddish. Finally in a barrage of exploding volcanoes, falling meteors, and disastrous super earthquakes, most of mankind is destroyed.

This scenario of events has been foretold in the Bible. It repeats similar events that can be witnessed in other parts of the universe, and that has already happened many times in Earth's 5.5 billion years of existence, in a universe estimated at 12-15 billion years old. In the Biblical span of time, "A day in the time of God is like a thousand years to mankind", which may not be literal, as a day in God's time may be a billion years to humans, using scientific facts.

The Kuiper Asteroid Belt is filled with millions of asteroids in dynamic random collisions. We need not wait for an errant asteroid resulting from planetary collision from other galaxies. A 10-mile wide asteroid, very small by astronomical standards, is sufficient to bring mass extinction on Earth. A 100 mile wide asteroid, heavy in iron content, would be much faster than a bullet, traveling at least 50,000 miles per hour could punch it's way through the earth's crust, and cause magma to spew out from the earth, to cause the "sky be darkened, and the sun to appear as if looking through a sackcloth" at high noon. An asteroid of 500 miles or more in diameter most certainly would break the Earth into various chunks, exploding it as a bullet does when fired at an apple. Horrific? Yes! Unlikely? I wouldn't bet against it, because, it's not a matter of "IF", but

"WHEN". As the Bible attests, "No one knows the exact moment when the end comes, only God." But God has given us signs that the impending time of calamity draws near.

The Mayan calendar ceased in 2012 and some feared the end of the world... obviously that didn't happen. The Mayans worshipped Satan, with demonic blood sacrifices, and serpentine ornament and idols. And while we won't know the exact moment when Biblically predicted events will occur, the year 2012 may be the line drawn in the sand, as Satan himself challenges God to battle at Armageddon. Exactly when God will send Jesus and his angels to attack Satan, not even Satan knows. But once again, Lucifer has already issued the challenge to God. Don't be surprised to witness weird looking space ships to descend from the skies, with the power to torment and destroy Satan's followers. And seeing an "alien" invasion from outer space, mankind will launch his nuclear arsenal, but to no avail. He shall lose against the all-powerful Annunaki Gods of the heavens from their outer space mother ship.

Meanwhile, we are each given an individual choice to choose good over evil, to stop worshipping the things Lucifer places before us, like money, greed, sex, alcohol, drugs, envy, hatred, and other situations that take our focus from serving a just and righteous God. But it is a difficult and narrow path to walk, that singular path to eternal salvation. The path is wide for the hoards that follow Satan to their doom. We have not but another decade to prepare and strengthen ourselves for the ultimate final battle between good and evil. Satan will force each one of us to choose between he and God. It is foretold that being Christian will be dangerous, but those who are strong and fear not death in this world, shall reap everlasting life in heaven on board their cube.

Chapter 2 - Philosophical paradigm shift

Our ancestors who hunted and gathered for subsistence probably enjoyed their lives without the daily pressures and frustration modern people endure in their daily lives. Current social norms dictate that a person's worth is in proportion to productivity as evidenced by socioeconomic status, material accumulation and financial net worth. A person without a job, business, homeownership and a late model car is generally considered a "loser" who deserves little if any respect. Over 70% of American workers live month to month, paycheck to paycheck and less than a third have sufficient savings to last six months of unemployment. The success paradigm is not working for most Americans, of whom at least 70% are willing to anonymously admit they dislike or even hate their jobs for various reasons that include insufficient wages, obnoxious demanding bosses, back stabbing co-workers who are "slackers" and unfulfilling work related tasks unrelated to educational attainment.

There are many other reasons why Americans find their careers, family lives, and other relationships to be unsatisfactory and in many cases miserable. The divorce rate in America exceeds 50%, so while homosexual couples are fighting to get marriage rights, married heterosexuals are fighting in divorce courts. Probably half of those who do not divorce are living lives of compromise in order to stay together for their minor children or to avoid the drama of property settlements and child custody battles. There's an old adage that states, "It's cheaper to keep her" and this point of wisdom has proven true in very public celebrity divorces, such as that endured by Tiger Woods after his ex-wife discovered his multitude of mistresses.

The philosophical paradigm that the vast majority of Americans have accepted as reality is generally comprised of a couple dozen core beliefs, including:

- There's such a thing as good and evil, right and wrong
- There are facts in the real world that are obvious for all to see

- The foundation of success is earning money in a career
- Freedom and independence is a fundamental right
- We should strive to do our best, to reach our full potential
- Charity, kindness, love, sacrifice and forgiveness are essential acts
- Violence is bad, but you have a right to defend yourself and family
- Heroes are those who put themselves in harms way for others
- Being popular is generally as important or more so than being smart
- Celebrity following, worship and emulation
- A college degree equates to social validation and financial success
- Being very attractive is as important or more so than being charitable
- Sports spectators identify with teams as if they are apart of them
- Being wealthy is better than being educated, smart, or admired
- Anger management and control of sexual urges is fundamental
- Nice guys usually come in last, but they're non-threatening
- Real men are expected to be strong and don't cry
- Bigger and more is almost always better than the opposite
- Risk taking increases the odds of greater thrills, fun and success
- The best activities are those that are enjoyable and fun to do
- Honesty and trustworthiness are good character traits to possess
- Everyone wants to be happy and fulfilled
- Life is the most valuable right anyone can have
- People don't have a right to determine when they want to die

The preponderance of evidence indicates the vast majority of people subscribe to most of these ideas and ideals as being the operative principles in reality. However, let's take a look at whether behavior actually correspond to ideals, or are people basically giving lip service to illusions seen through tinted glasses? Let's examine some of these social norms:

- If there exist good and evil, right and wrong, then why is it that when situations or results are not self-serving and beneficial or result in a loss of personal assets, then it's wrong and bad – even though others may derive greater benefits, and vice versa good is when there is sufficient self-benefits. The idea of good and bad as an absolute value is mostly a subjective personal judgment that may or may not conform to social norms, political correctness or group think... but people will pretend by giving lip service in support of such nebulous notions.

- If facts are so obvious for all to see, then why do a significant number of people believe the 911 collapse of the WTC twin towers in NYC was in fact a conspiracy involving our military industrial complex and high levels of government? Why did FDR let the Japanese bomb Pearl Harbor without warning our troops when they already intercepted Japanese communications and broke their code a month prior to Pearl Harbor? Why do people politely and disingenuously complement others for their fashions and appearance when they don't believe it?

- If the foundation of success is earning money in a career, then why are the wealthiest people often without college degrees who started their own businesses, rather than to work for someone else?

- Freedom and independence is a fundamental right, but there are laws against everything in all aspects of people's lives to mandate conformity.

- We should strive to do our best, to reach our full potential and get all stressed out chasing that elusive potential. People are all born with varying degrees of talent, intelligence, memory, and desire. Most people can never reach an apex level of achievement, ever. And even at their best, it may be a paltry "also ran" compared to the alpha achievers.

- If charity, kindness, love, sacrifice and forgiveness are essential acts, then why do the preponderance of people spend almost all of their time and resources on themselves?

- Violence is bad, but you have a right to defend yourself and family using violence, and to kill others if you feel your life or that of your loved ones are being threatened… it's a Second Amendment justification for gun ownership, up to and including assault rifles designed to kill people.

- Heroes are those who put themselves in harms way for others at great peril to their own lives, but the term is getting watered down when people who suffer diseases, hardships, and injuries are called heroes for enduring suffering instead of killing themselves to avoid more misery.

- Being popular is usually more important than being smart because social success has a market value that can translate to improved career positions and higher levels of prestige.

- People want to copy and celebrate the stars, but just as easily will jump on the band wagon to destroy them when they falter, then substitute their supposed undying loyalty and worship to other rich and famous celebrities admired by other brainless followers, just to fit in.

- A college degree is usually worthless except in highly technical and scientific fields. College degrees have become so common place that most jobs actually utilize very little of what college graduates learn in their courses. Instead, employers often tell grads to forget what they learned in school in order to train to the methods and standards that are required in the real world of employment success.

- Being very attractive is far more important than being kind because it opens doors in certain fields because attractive people more in demand and thus more valuable. Why else is personal expenditures on beauty products, clothing and surgery more than 1000 times than that given to charitable causes?

- Sports spectators who feel team loyalties have been known to fight and start riots in demonstrating their team devotion, but if they're really part of the teams rather than mindless emotional spectators vicariously rooting for people who don't know them, wouldn't want to know them, and don't care if they rooted for another team, then why aren't they being paid?

- Being wealthy beats being educated, smart, admired, talented or anything else. Period. Those who deny this reality only do so because they are not wealthy so don't enjoy the perks that wealth can bring, versus minimal negatives if wealth and emotional needs are wisely managed.

- Anger management and control of sexual urges is required to live among other people, but were there no law enforcement in society, the apex predators would routinely be getting away with rape and murder.

- Nice guys do come in last, only because females have been brainwashed by media to desire the type of physical men whose primary focus is on themselves. Nice guys are usually seen as friends without any sexual benefits, but they are loyal and will listen to all the sob stories women have about the guys they love. Something's not adding up here.

- Real men are expected to be strong and not to cry in the face of danger and tragedy, otherwise be disrespected as wimps. But in moments of privacy, women love to see the tender side of their men if it exists at all.

- Bigger and more is better. Large breasts, long strong thick penises, and for some, large posteriors is always better. Big bank accounts is best.

- Taking big risks increases the odds of greater thrills, fun and success is the rationale for those who survive jumping off cliffs, riding motorcycles over 150 mph, and investing in heavily leveraged companies or make large gambling bets. It doesn't count all those who crash and burn.

- The best activities are those that are enjoyable and fun to do. I guess that's why volunteering to clean house for the disabled isn't one of the top choices. Video games, spectator sports, boozing, Internet porn and wasting time talking about nonsense with family and friends is popular.

- Honesty and trustworthiness are good character traits to possess, but too often are taken advantaged of by those who don't ascribe to such values. Honest people often wear a scarlet letter "S" for stupid as a sucker is born every minute. Predators and manipulators know that.

- Everyone wants to be happy and fulfilled but the experience is so highly subjective that most people settle for the joy of materialism and getting the latest high tech gadgets that they can really live without, except they convince themselves that they can't be happy without their toys.

- Life is the most valuable right anyone can have, and that's why there's poverty because it's better to be poor and starving than to be dead. I wonder if sometimes how often those who suffer life the most think of dying as a release from the chains of barely surviving.

- People don't have a right to determine when they want to die because suicide and voluntary euthanasia is illegal. Government, doctors, and family members reserve the right to make life or death decisions for people, but the individual does not have that right when they're bedridden in a coma on life support as a result of an accident or illness. The standard procedure is to "pull the plug" to save insurance companies tons of expensive critical care after doctors convince family members that recovery is highly improbable. Then if the patients family desires to cash in on large insurance policies, they're more likely to consent to an overdose of morphine (for the pain of course) that causes respiratory arrest and a supposed peaceful death... only how can we be sure?

Let's focus on several of the primary philosophical issues that are usually high on the list of people's lives... happiness, death and the order of things.

The Happiness Paradigm

HAPPINESS... almost everyone born wants it, seeks it, and cherishes it. Our U.S. Constitution guarantees our PURSUIT OF HAPPINESS. But to most people, happiness is usually a fleeting illusion, or distant memories of silly childhood innocence. Happiness means many things to many people. Whether rich or poor, intelligent or stupid, well educated or illiterate, mean or nice, or whatever in between, the common goal in life comes down to HAPPINESS. The problem with modern society appears to be, the more we have, the less happy people seem to get.

Perhaps trying to be happy in a world that has become too complex has its drawbacks. Maybe it's too difficult to find the simple happiness buried under layers of mental and emotional clutter, which has been defined by our social conditioning and cultural norms. Certainly, happiness is oftentimes to be found right under our noses. And it's usually free for the discovery, if we could only see it clearly.

Let's first look at what external and superficial things most people have equated with happiness, and look at those situations that makes them either happy or miserable. To a vast majority of people in our consumerist and materialistic society, happiness means, among other things:

- Winning at various games
- Owning things that others admire, like a nice car, clothes, home, boat, or other name brand items or status symbols
- Money, and lots of it; wealth
- Being appreciated and acknowledged by people they value
- Coming out relatively unscathed from a harrowing experience like a horrific car or plane crash or a wild fire.
- Freedom to do as one pleases without impediments and barriers
- Obtaining benefits with little or no effort, such as getting something free, or at a bargain price
- Contributing positively to improve other people's lives
- Obtaining deserved recognition, credit, advancement, and opportunities
- Taking advantage of others through clever manipulation
- Being inspired by the positive examples and sacrifices of others
- Achieving one's personal plans, goals, and objectives
- Discovering something new; knowledge, perception, or situation
- Pleasurable experiences, feelings, thoughts or stimuli
- Belonging to a sense of something bigger than oneself, a cause or group
- Appreciating natural surroundings
- A general love for living things and people
- Self-empowerment and/or power over others
- Successfully hurting one's enemies or revenge

- Creativity
- Destruction
- Humor and laughter
- Recreational activities
- Fulfilling relationships
- Sumptuous food and/or drink
- Bodily comfort and contact
- Emotional connectivity; love
- Avoiding punishment for wrongdoings
- Finding a loved one or something values that was lost
- Discovering and practicing one's spirituality
- These are but a small fraction of some of the multitude of specific things that seem to make different people happy at various times in their lives.
- The commonality that is apparent in various measures of happiness is self-benefit. The person who perceives and feels happiness is able to derive a sense of achievement and satisfaction, whether that comes from material or intangible sources. To some, it's based primarily on money and what it can buy, but with others, it's all about the gratitude and appreciation received from others. Still others are happiest through the tangible results of their effort to improve the lives of the less fortunate.
- It appears the opportunity for happiness abound. Then why are so man people unhappy so much of the time? Many attempts have been made to try to explain why people are unhappy and/or depressed. Observations have resulted in the coining of such clichés as "Misery loves company," "Nobody wants a loser," "Everybody loves a winner," "Be careful what you wish for, it may come true," and many other ominous notions of wisdom.

Anyone who has had been around infants, toddlers, and young children notices how happy most of them seem most of the time. Something happens around the age of 5, which incidentally coincides with parental separation and the beginning of public school rigors and the academic grading system. Yet for all the focus on teaching and grading our young, the universal result has been a loss of happiness, increased rebelliousness, and oftentimes, social alienation and anti-social feelings and behavior. Ask most people who have been products of our education system, and we find that they've forgotten at least 95% of what they had supposedly learned in school, and find that 99% of what they had to endure to learn in school has become irrelevant in their adult lives. The only thing that seems to linger on a general sense of insecurity and fear of being judged, ridiculed, or punished for being less than what is expected by authority figures or the social norms. Certainly there are many reasons and experiences that begin to rob a person of their happiness such that happy and innocent children eventually evolve into grumpy and cynical elder people. There are several areas that fundamentally change a person's development and perception of happiness, which create life-long attitudes and predispose people to lingering unhappiness and discontentment.

How can we help our children to develop into happy and enriched people? One area that can be addressed is the education system. We are all products of the social conditioning that occurs at school, and appear to retain more of the socialization and normative values than the academic facts. We do as much learning about our society and its expectations and values during lunch breaks as we do during classroom instruction. For example, we learn which people are more popular, and those attributes that are socially rewarded, which usually reflects media hype, fictional television shows, and television commercial that create artificial needs and desires.

We learn who are the "cool" kids, the nerds, and weirdoes, and the rejects. These social perceptions become life long stereotypes and values that limit our ability to accept ourselves or others for who they really are. In fact, too many people go through life not really knowing who they are, but simply struggling to fulfill social norms, to avoid rejection, ridicule, and prejudice. Why are people spending billions of dollars on dieting? Is it for the intrinsic health value, or is the motivation based primarily on "looking good" to attain social acceptance?

The question arises, why is it necessary or desirable to create a social structure that categories and divides people into different levels of value and importance? Why are niches created, where a person's sense of self-worth and happiness depends upon social stature and materialism? The fact remains that a hierarchical and differentiated social structure exists in almost all current societies among human beings. Anthropologists and sociologist may not agree on the degree of hereditary predisposition versus learned values as contributing causes to social organization; however, as individuals living in societies that we did not design, we're stuck with it and it's not likely to change anytime soon.

Now, what can we do as individuals to alter our own realities, in order to permit us to pursue our personal happiness, within the social context that we are allowed? First, let's recognize how fortunate we Americans are to live in a relatively free society, where our basic liberties are protected by laws. But as our society and laws become more complex, inconsistent, and even contradictory, much confusion arises as to what freedoms and liberties define.

Let's look at several basic premises that are universal components to the pursuit of personal happiness in our society, as in any society in our world.

- Freedom of choice
- Self direction, expression, and acceptance
- Freedom from repressive controls and manipulation by others
- Positive human relations

- Avoidance of punishment
- Getting what you want
- Basic humanitarian needs fulfillment and human dignity
- Positive mental and emotional attitude and orientation
- Positive living environment
- Ability to solve problems in a constructive manner
- These universal components to pursuing individual happiness do not require excesses in monetary or material things, and can be achievable with little or no effort, so long as the social structure permits and encourages individual freedom and liberty.
- Why are people not happy with their lives in general, or happy more often? Besides the socialized niches and categories that have already befallen us through the education-indoctrination system, media brainwashing, and negative life experiences (such as overly punitive legal/court system), the apparent lack of opportunities and life options, and other dynamics spawned by special interest governance, people find themselves being pulled apart on a daily basis by competing and complex demands on their time and energy. People become so busy with life's demands, they don't find time to be happy.
- Let's take a closer look at how we can take constructive steps to enjoy the eight universal components that comprise the foundation of personal happiness.

Freedom of Choice.

Rules are everywhere, and few remember why they were made, and who made them in the first place. Oftentimes, rules were made because people who had authority and power over others felt compelled to structure how people should behave in a particular place and situation. Freedom of choice is stifled for the convenience of the majority or a few who are in control.

In order to maximize freedom of choice, it is often essential to decide to accept the consequences of one's situation. Alternatively, many people attempt to circumvent the rules, which creates punitive responses and more conflict. Otherwise, a happier option would be to withdraw from situations where one does not agree with the rules, and go somewhere else that has situations that present more freedom of choice and fewer rules.

If you don't like your situation, change it, or move on. If you can't change it, then change yourself, or move on. If it's not worth your time and effort to change, then move on. Untold millions of people find themselves in predicaments where social norms, company rules, or legal constraints make them feel boxed in. Consequently, too many people sacrifice their happiness and remain in miserable marriages, oppressive jobs, or over-regulated cities and states. Surprisingly, people remain in these miserable situations, and some finally snap and end up on the nightly news as a homicide suspect, or arrested for actions that could have been avoided, if only they changed their residence by as little as a few blocks.

Self-direction, expression, and acceptance.

Most people don't enjoy being told what to do, when or where to go, or how to achieve something. People naturally resist being controlled, and this instinct goes far beyond teen-age rebelliousness. No one can know what's best for another person because no one knows the inner workings, feelings, beliefs, and social conditioning of another. Everybody has their own path in life, and no one else can walk in another person's shoes while they're still in them. The only observation others can make is to see another's footprints in the sand, which is only an external and superficial indication of another's path. Consequently, happiness is increased when people seek their own paths, recognizing that on one else can know better about oneself, than oneself. Why worry about what other people think, since they are likely to be inaccurate, wrong, or simply serving their own agendas or belief systems. *To thyself be true!* Find your own path. No one can feel your happiness or misery except you. It takes too much effort to be a fake person in order to fit in or to please others. It's always much simpler and more gratifying to accept yourself for who you really are. Be honest and be happy.

Freedom from repressive controls and manipulation by others.

Everyday that we wake, drive to and from work or school, and have contact with the public, co-workers, bosses, and family, it is likely we will run into a rude, inconsiderate and toxic person. There exist that 10% (or more) of people whose personalities are abrasive because they discovered early on that it increases the percentage of times that they can get their way. They are not concerned about what other people feel, think, want, desire or are entitled to obtain. The concept of fairness, cooperation, kindness, and consideration does not exist in the minds and hearts of these types of problematic and aggressive *"Type A"* people.

The best way to deal with these demanding troublemakers is to avoid them as soon as you recognize them coming your way. Never let yourself work for one of them, or God forbid get entwined in an intimate relationship with these manipulative and oppressive people. These *Type A* personalities never grew up emotionally from infancy, and are stuck on the *"It's mine"* and *"I want!"* stage of childhood development. Often, when these immature adults don't get their way, they will be impatient and display anger, until someone nice comes along to placate them. You'll be a lot happier if you don't surround yourself with these mean spirited and destructive people. If you have them in your life, try real hard to lose them, before they make you a loser.

Positive human relations.

Man does not live by bread alone. No man is an island. Human beings are instinctively social animals, and need other people for company, stimulation, and relationships. All people get lonely from time to time, and the surest cure for loneliness and alienation is the company of positive friends, families, and strangers. Sharing meaningful and enjoyable experiences bring joy and lighten one's emotional and mental loads. Computer gadgets, cell phones, and the Internet has greatly extended relationship building into our fantasy realm, where cyber friends can now fulfill a significant portion of relationship building, with less exposure to potentially negative aspects of entanglement. At the same time, the Internet offers an expanded format for meeting others, and many have found great connections from communicating on-line with others through social media.

Avoidance of punishment.

With the exception of masochists, few people enjoy punishment and pain. People will go to great lengths to avoid penalties and negative consequences for their mistakes, poor behavior, or criminal activities. Most people will lie, exaggerate, withhold information, and blame others long before admitting something, in attempting to avoid paying fines, being ridiculed, hearing disapproval and criticism, possible incarceration, or other potential personal losses such as one's job or intimate relationship. Sometimes, admission is the best policy, because it clears one's conscience and releases one from the trap of having to tell more lies to cover up for the previous lies. The best remedy is to avoid behavior, speech, activities, situations, people, or environment that increase one's exposure to negative consequences, that come with penalties or punishment. Teen-agers who hang out with the wrong crowd are just waiting for something bad to happen. People who *think before they leap* greatly improve their chances of avoiding punishment because they would more likely refrain from actions that come at a very high price.

Getting what you want.

Almost everyone instinctively wants to reach their goals, whether their objectives are immediate, short, or long-term. After infancy and upon entering Kindergarten and onward, people soon discover that it becomes highly problematic and difficult to get one's way very often. The reason is due to the *freeway paradigm*. Anyone who has driven in Los Angeles soon learns about freeway traffic slowing to a crawl during its notorious rush hours that is punctuated by stop and go traffic. When many more people share limited space and resources, your progress is going to suffer because you're in direct competition with others with similar goals. Traffic also comes in clusters because several inconsiderate drivers will intentionally or stupidly form a moving roadblock to keep everyone else behind them (sometimes it's just a power trip). Freedom and rapid progress is only possible when you maneuver around these clusters; but after a very short run, you will invariable find yourself sucking in the exhaust from the next cluster of vehicles.

Life is like freeway traffic. During rush hour, it's probably best to use alternate routes because there are too many people on the highway. Otherwise be prepared to be frustrated, late for dinner, or your favorite television show. If you can figure out the timing of the traffic lights on certain streets, you can make real progress without the overcrowded freeways. Getting one's way greatly depends on *good timing*, and *minimizing competition*, and the ability to *maneuver around obstacles*. The better you are at recognizing traffic patterns and trends, the greater are your chances for getting your way and making real progress in your life.

Basic humanitarian needs fulfillment and human dignity.

Basic needs must be fulfilled before we can feel a sense of happiness. Few people can feel a sense of joy when they're starving, thirsty, weak, oppressed, cold, and in pain. A person can't be happy when they see their loved ones in pain, poor health, oppressed, malnourished, or miserable. Having one's basic needs met – food, shelter, health, intimacy, and income source does not automatically make a person happy, because once this level of need has been fulfilled, it is usually expected and taken for granted. However, when basic needs are not met, worry, unhappiness, and discontent rapidly sets in and become formidable barriers to happiness. A building without a strong foundation is always threatened by sudden and catastrophic collapse. Take care of your basic needs first, or you won't last.

Positive mental and emotional attitude and orientation.

Is the glass "half full" or "half empty"? Would you be depressed at losing a leg from a devastating accident, or be glad you didn't lose either legs or your life instead? Do you laugh at ridiculous and rude people, or let them ruin your day? Can you be satisfied with what you've got, or is it never enough, no matter what? Are you happy only when you "win", or does evidence of progress sufficient to thrill you? Do you feel a sense of failure if you don't achieve what you plan, or do you feel each attempt places you closer to your goals? Are you usually jealous and envious of what others have? Do you feel angry because you don't feel you have obtained your "just" deserves? Do you think life is not fair? Do you feel lucky, or cursed by bad luck?

A person's attitude is probably the greatest determinant of feeling happy or dissatisfied. Life is not fair! It never has been, and never will be. Some people will always have more, and others will have to do with much less. There is not such thing as true *equality*. Never has been, and never will be. Everyone's circumstances and situations are unique to them. No two persons can fit in the same shoes at the same time. If we accept from life what it gives us, and be thankful that we received anything at all, instead of expecting more and more, we can release ourselves from unnecessary pressure, misery and disappointments. Having plans, goals, and a direction in life is nice, but if they're not realistic and don't reflect your true desires, maybe it's time to reassess what it would take to make your truly happy.

Positive living environment.

If you live in a pigpen, around pigs, you'd likely smell, look, and sound like a pig. If you want to be miserable, commit a serious crime and get locked up in jail. If you want to be happy, find a happy place in the world, around happy people, doing things that make you happy.
Too many people fall into the "comparison trap", which sets people up for a rough roller coaster ride, trying to keep up with or surpass others. If you define your happiness based upon what other people do, feel, believe, own, or say, you are letting others determine whether you could or should be happy. Happiness is not a *zero-sum game*. There isn't a limited amount of happiness in the world. Instead, like misery, happiness abounds and is unlimited.

The only person who can limit your true happiness is yourself. You must recognize that in this world and in this life, no one really cares too much about you once you're no longer a cute innocent toddler. You're basically on your own to obtain your own benefits and to try to avoid pain and misfortune. NO BODY OWES YOU A LIVING, AND NO ONE IS OBLIGATED TO MAKE YOU HAPPY! In the real world, it's the survival of the fittest, so try to find an environment where you can flourish, and not be eaten by the beasts.

Ability to solve problems in a constructive manner.

The schools are fairly good for teaching students what they really don't want to know, and very poor at teaching them what they need to know to survive and be happy in the real world. By 7 years old, most children have decided whether they want to learn based upon their treatment at school by their teachers and peers. Academic grading, and *grading on a curve* sets into motion a series of life altering experiences that is apt to create 9 failures for every success. Only a score of 90% earns a child an "A", then everything else is considered "less than", which in our *winning* obsesses society is synonymous with *losing*. It's sad, but the result of schooling is the creation of failures. Even if a children were to try their very best, and could only muster up a 59% score (that's like knowing 6 out of 10 answers), they will receive a BIG FAT FAIL, AN "F". It's no wonder after a few strings of failure scores that children begin to believe they are in fact failures, and give up trying. It's only logical. Why bust your butt to become a failure, when failing is free? Hey, who's smarter here? The school system or the student? Instead of producing masses upon masses of faceless failures to place into society as a directionless mulch, our education system need to do a much better job teaching our children how to make good decisions in their lives. We need children who grow into well-adjusted adults who are capable of analyzing real world problems, and possess the creativity to solve them.

Unfortunately, what we're getting out of our schools for all the tax dollars is a system that attempts to make everyone into cows, to be herded from corral to corral at the appropriate times for feeding and crapping. Only in relatively few schools are children instilled with a thirst for life-long learning, where their lessons are applicable to real life.

How many college graduates earn their degrees, only to find their knowledge to be irrelevant to the jobs and careers that they eventually attempt? I would venture to state, the vast majority! When I graduated from college, my first job as a manager trainee used little of the vast stores of knowledge I had accrued from 4 years of brain drain. I was told by the manager to forget everything I learned in college about business principles, because he wanted to train me the way things really work in the real world of making profits.

After completing my masters degree program, I soon discovered that agencies were looking for people with real world experiences, and my three-year trek and hard work to earn a masters degree was given the same weight as one additional year of work experience. Hey, with simple math like that, maybe college students are kind of stupid. College graduates enter the work world in debt, and are unlikely to be hired for a job that would allow them to pay off their student loans. Instead, anyone who is 18 years old can take a few courses, pass a few exams, and obtain a certificate or license that permits them to earn a six figure income in real estate, stockbrokerage, construction, sales, retail management, insurance, and a dozen other fields.

It's common knowledge among entrepreneurs and businessmen that college graduates make good technicians, if they have a technical background in engineering, science, finance, accounting or computers. Otherwise, the "A" college students usually end up working as a professional for a manager who was a "B" student, and all work for a college drop out who was a "C" student, who had to survive, so started a thriving business that grew into a corporation.

Our schools and colleges are turning out generations of underachievers who have been sold a BIG FAT LIE. We all know that in almost every career and organization, superstars are a threat to the status quo, unless they are selling something, or somehow adding directly to the bottom line. All others are just taking up space that will eventually be used for the new upgraded computers.

Let's just teach our children how to get along, how to solve real world problems, how to be honest and ethical in their lives, how to be the good parents that they probably never had, then give them the option to choose what types of things they really want to learn, so they can enjoy their learning, and actually strive to reach their potential for happiness. You must also recognize that no matter how carefully and thoughtfully you prepared your plans, *Murphy's Law* waits around the next corner. Shit happens from time to time, and usually at the worse possible moments.

But it doesn't mean the game is over, because you can always wash the crap off yourself, and end up smelling rosy once again. All storms eventually come to an end, and though it may feel very rough while you're trying to ride it out, trying not to drown, at least a storm brings plenty of water. Water is necessary for life to survive and grow, so the next time a storm visits your life, take a bucket out and drink; otherwise your complaints might be heard by the rain Gods, who may decide to cast you into the valley of drought.

DON'T WORRY. BE HAPPY! Be happy for what you have. Don't worry because you can't live another second in life until it comes. You can't borrow time from the future, and pay it back at a later date. Try to live every second, every minute, every hour, and every day of your life, as if it may be your last. For as certain as the sun eventually shines, the next second you live could be your last. So why not enjoy your last moments in life while you still can?

Let's summarize the process of being happy. Being happy is a rather simple proposition and process. First, you have to really want it. Then you have to know what it feels like, what it smells and taste like. Then you have to put yourself into an environment, in situations, and around people who can bring you joy. Finally, you have to recognize and appreciate happiness when it comes your way, and realize that it's always just where you can't see it, and where you're not looking; in your mind and in your heart. If you're not happy after all that, then you can always enjoy other people's misery, because *misery loves company!* Best wishes to you in your pursuit of happiness!

HOW TO BE HAPPY AS OFTEN AS POSSIBLE

- No drama, conflict, arguments or violence
- No bureaucratic harassment or intimidation
- No insincere and hidden agendas from people
- Situations that reward honesty, truthfulness and loyalty
- Feeling freedom from victimization
- Freedom from censorship of freedom of speech
- Freedom of spiritual contemplation, prayer and worship
- People to honor their commitments and agreements
- Freedom of expression, activities, and personal privacy
- Minimal social, family or employer pressure and demands
- Civil, courteous, kind, considerate and polite people
- Freedom from physical, mental, or emotional suffering
- Opportunities to contribute to improving society
- Helping those in need, and not users, abusers, rip offs,
- opportunists, and predators
- Self-improvement and skills development
- Educational opportunities, classes, learning, and enrichment
- Occasional intimacy, romance and honest relationship
- No fears, anxieties, obsessions, addictions or compulsions

- Comfort in knowing family & loved ones are healthy & safe
- Comfortable and secure home and community
- Financial security & legal money-making opportunities through career, employment, or entrepreneurship
- Entertaining past times, events and hobbies, including:
  a. Meaningful and nice social interactions and company
  b. Sports activities and spectatorship
  c. Natural surroundings; beach, lake, or mountains
  d. Museums of all types
  e. Motorcycling and scenic relaxing drives
  f. Good movies and television programs
  g. Enriching Internet surfing for discovery & exploring views
  h. Art, music, photography, sculpture, poetry, and pottery
  i. Writing essays, web building, emails, postings and blogs
  j. Email to make social contacts
  k. Petition in support of social activism
  l. Video games and amusement rides
  m. Fishing, hunting, boating, camping and recreation
  n. Beer drinking but not drunkenness
  o. University environment
  p. Libraries

Obstacles to the Attainment of Happiness

1. Living with negative, critical, abusive, selfish bi-polar nut case people
2. Employed in negative, stressful, back-stabbing & violent career
3. Living in a gang-infested low socio-economic neighborhood
4. Earning unpredictable and low income
5. No career advancement potential with unpredictable future
6. No health and dental insurance coverage
7. Low financial and career motivation or desire for monetary gain

8.   Cynical and futile worldview on people, govt., culture and society

9.   Family and friendship pressure and demands on my time & effort

10. No constructive personal relationships, benefactors or mentors

11. Physical injuries, deteriorating health, and suffering

Possible Solutions to Obstacles to Happiness

- [#1-8 are job or income dependent]

- Live alone or with new college aged gal pal(s) or buddy(ies)
- New F/T job in good location with mellow & honest boss
- Move to better and safer neighborhood
- New F/T job with P/T back-up income
- New F/T job with advancement opportunities
- New F/T job with career satisfaction opportunities
- New F/T job with employee benefits coverage
- New F/T job with worthwhile tasks
- Withdraw from new issues and read positive materials
- Minimize contact with demanding family members
- Internet search for compatible friends and mates
- Get depression treatment, exercise, and drink less beer

Chronology for Improving Life (examples of monthly goals)

April	New P/T weekend job
May	Join Real Estate firm P/T
June	Obtain good F/T job
July	Find better and safer neighborhood & move
Aug	Lover goes her own way and we remain friends
Sept	Make new friends with positive people
Oct	Pursue on-line masters degree
Nov	Resolve masters degree program

| Dec | Begin gym exercise plan |
| Jan | Start web-based business |

As with most things in life, the ease at which goals are expected to be accomplished are usually underestimated, and the obstacles and unseen challenges to achievement are magnified due to the decisions and actions of others involved. But in this case, the time line was reasonable and all goals were accomplished, though not exactly in the order as planned or to the degree of success as envisioned. Nevertheless, the achievement of the goals were progressive steps toward personal validation, fulfillment, and happiness that is essentially a matter of attitude. I was always astonished when T.V. news reports indicated super wealthy people were committing suicide or drug overdosed. Now, "who woulda thunk" that people with the financial means to have privileges, property, comforts, travel, and all the amenities of "the good life" could be unhappy enough to kill themselves? They must have been very miserable, R.I.P.

Aspect	%Importance	% Desire	%Achieved	% Deficit
purpose	100	100	50	50
meaning	100	100	40	60
happiness	90	90	50	40
serenity	90	80	40	40
peace	80	90	30	60
true love	80	80	20	60
acceptance	60	70	60	10
success	70	80	55	30
enjoyment	80	80	40	40
escape	60	75	30	45
romance	70	75	30	45
praise	50	60	50	10
friendship	60	70	20	50
achievement	80	85	70	15
changes	80	95	30	65
financial	90	95	40	55
creativity	80	70	60	10
inventiveness	80	80	70	10
freedom	90	100	60	40
loyalty	70	95	45	50
vehicles	80	85	35	50
travel	70	95	40	55
nice home	70	75	30	45
technology	70	80	35	45
entertainment	80	85	45	40
Total Average	7.68	84	43	41

After analyzing and tracking the various aspects of self-validation, social validation, emotional needs, cultural and social norms, instinctive desires, distractions, entertainment, plans, goals, and whatever I thought would make me feel alive and fulfilled, I found that I fell quite short of attaining that elusive "sweet spot" in life, achieving less than half of what I thought were important aspects of my life. So is the glass "half full" or half empty?

Psychic ability and intuition are terms that are often misunderstood and used interchangeably to explain the world around us when we are not satisfied with our state of affairs. Notions such as fate, déjà vu, luck, divine purpose and other spiritual and pseudo-scientific explanations are often proposed to explain or justify people's predicaments and outcomes.

1. Do we inadvertently attract to us people and situations based upon our thoughts?

    Answer - Yes; how much depends on intensity of emotions if consonant or dissonant to universal thought-stream resulting in directive positive or negative, or random results.

2. What are the proportionate effects of "strong" emotions on creating futures?

    Answer - Mathematical relations between intensity with consonance or dissonance with the planetary, solar system, galactic, universal spiritual [energy-matter-time conversion] flux.

3. Which are strong emotions and weak emotions?

    Answer - Fear, love, hate, desire, greed, sorrow, sympathy, arousal, anxiety, hopefulness can all be highly intense and applied to influence future outcomes.

4. Do dogs, animals, and people intuitively sense "fear" or "kindness" in people and respond accordingly?

    Answer - "Lower" animals adapted to predatory environments evolved keener "instincts" against natural dangers, thus can "sense" certain stronger emotions in people due to the biochemical release of certain scents [probably androgens, testosterone, adrenal and progesterone based secretions.

5. How can we attract positive futures?

    Answer - Recognize the timing and interaction of natural and worldly events and trends, the effects of strong emotions and thoughts and floating on the universal thought-stream river of cause/effect/destiny instead of fighting and trying to swim against the tide.

6. How do spirits affect us in the physical world?

Answer - Spirits co-exist with the physical plane & can observe but rarely effect physical objects; however when a "critical mass" of spirits act in unison, or very strong spirits exert focused energy, effects may result in the physical world.

7. Is the subconscious a gateway to the spiritual realm?

Answer - When the brain is deficient in certain areas due to synaptic dysfunction, other parts of the brain compensate, creating a private world when connections to the physical world is too difficult. Genius, creativity, and inventiveness readily exude from some people and perhaps some can perceive telepathy etc.

8. How can we be happy with our circumstances when we know it does not fulfill our desires or needs?

Answer - We can compare how better off our circumstances are versus prior situations, or to that of less fortunate, or how much worse it could be for the occurrence of negative outcomes of potential past or futures from which we are separated only by fractions of inches or seconds, or we can accept our circumstances as the present, the best of what could be at the moment (which has a 99 to 1 chance of being worse rather than better), then take progressive constructive steps to improve our situation towarddesired goals.

9. Is it possible to make telepathic suggestions to influence thoughts and actions in others?

Answer - Like most other facets of the physical world, 99% of the people are incapable for an assortment of reasons. The 1% who can accomplish this feat certainly aren't going to tell anyone for obvious reasons of fear, jealousy, distrust, and other human insecurities.

10. If we put certain thoughts into the "thought-stream", do people react or respond to it?

Answer - Yes. People who are sensitive to intuitive feelings and freeform thoughts are more likely to be better receptors (as those who are easily hypnotized). People who respond more to their subconscious minds rather than their conscious minds are more able to tune into the universal thought stream. Those who primarily deal with the conscious world framework tend to shut out thoughts that don't already respond and   conform to the parameters of their focus and singular orientation.

11. If we verbalize our thoughts, do the thoughts become stronger because it is put out into the physical realm thus enables others to react and respond?

Answer - Yes. the verbal reinforces the thought, creating physical world vibrations that are perceived by others more readily on the physical plane. That's why it's better to keep secret one's fondest plans and dreams so others are not given the chance to compete or to sabotage them.

12. How can we get spirits to work to our benefit?

Answer - First, we must not fear them, but realize that there are good and evil spirits, and all shades in between just as there are human personalities. As spirits, they have their needs and purpose in their spirit realm. The good spirits can help us only when our thoughts and feelings are good, thus their influence will be consonant with our souls

vibrations. the bad spirits need not be feared because while they have power, they are not able to harm us if the good spirits sent by God as connected by the Holy Spirit extends his protection. But when our souls are tarnished too much by evil in the physical realm, and we lose the spiritual connection to the goodness in our souls, then the evil spirits have much power to bring about negative outcomes to our realities.

13. Is fear the strongest emotional motivator? Is love and hate opposite reactions to fear?

Answer - Yes. The first natural instinct of babies or the young of any living thing is to imprint and depend on its parent for basic survival; however to become an independently surviving entity, fear becomes the first distinctly defined emotion that motivates humans toward seeking affiliation, family, friends and love. Fear also becomes the primary motivating factor for the development of hate which is aggression turned at potential or imagined enemies due to fear of harm.

14. Autohypnosis to affect subconscious habits and attitudes transforming   conscious realities?

Answer - Yes. But requires clarity of mind, a clean slate upon which to write new   behavioral instructions, thus must be meditative and clear of emotional and mental turmoil that would otherwise muck up the process.

15. How to recondition one's own thought processes to be more successful and happy.

Answer - Computer simulation model game. Imagine and visualize the process and   outcomes in all aspects of one's life as a holistic and integrated reality. Practice the game process repeatedly until it becomes habitual and positive outcomes are derived.

16. The theory of randomness and its applicability to life....
Evaluate life history... chance or plan?

Answer - Determine what events were due to chance, fate, choice/plan etc.,1/3 each?

17. Escapist activities to avoid dealing with unwanted, undesirable, unfulfilling realities?

Answer - Alcohol, drugs, sex, partying, night clubbing are usually bad. Movies, sports, television, and hobbies are usually constructive.

18. Methods to attract undamaged no drama females; break down

    Answer - Teens, early 20's, mid-late 20's, 30's 40's depending on looks, brains, &   family background.

19. More efficient use of spare time in desirable activities vs. escapist.

    Answer - One hour/day on Internet; one hour/day on freebies take on-line classes   reflect & read past thoughts read publication books do research on wealthy people

20. Are we able to effect physical health with thoughts and emotions?

    Answer - Body sensitivity is the first stage of mental/emotional awareness of the physical plane, which may alter body condition by mental instructions on cellular level that adjusts the type, and concentration of biochemical processes that affect health and disease. Much of effects may be related to subconscious and unresolved conflicts that either punish or reward the body for mental/emotional perceptions. The body naturally seeks homeostasis but the mental/emotional states usually acts to create unbalance due to conditioned and reactionary dysfunctions.

21. Are we able to create luck and fortune in terms of monetary gains by use of thoughts?

    Answer - There are several factors that cause "luck", whether good or bad. When the positive aspects are in consonance, "good luck" results. When bad aspects coincide, bad luck results. Mental, emotional, and subconscious beliefs must be in tune with the spiritual thought-stream and the intentions must be good in purpose to influence and direct the randomness of luck into a focused stream.

22. What activities help to clear the mind/emotions/body of toxins?
Answer -   First, the body must feel a sense of healthiness, life,
and fullness and be free of pain by sufficiently moderate
sustenance of water, food, and rest. A moderate level of physical
activities and exertion should adequately tone the body. The mind
thirsts for water [questions], food [answers] and rest [sleep &
dreams].

TIME MANAGEMENT DAILY SCHEDULE PARADIGM

Modern life in the cities comes with additional challenges, such as
rush hour grid lock while trying to get to work on time. Time management
has become an important overriding aspect that impacts our lives filled with
too many responsibilities and not enough time left in the day. A simple
general routine schedule may help to sort out daily activities and priorities
to minimize anxiety and stress from not knowing what to expect or what to
do in the course of managing time.

Developing a general daily routine allows certain repetitious tasks
to be placed on "automatic" mode that increases consistency and efficient
time management. For example, a simple daily schedule could be:

7:00 = WAKE UP/SSS
7:30 = GO TO ASSIGNED SCHOOL
8:00 = TEACH SPECIAL ED KIDS
2:30 = TEACHING DONE; GO HOME
3:00 = READ EMAIL/REST
3:30 = WEBSURF
4:30 = READ OR WRITE PROJECTS
6:30 = DINNER + TV
7:00 = TV, FREENET, MUSIC & TALK
10:00 = TV NEWS
11:00 = GO TO SLEEP

There are people who regularly impact our time, and it's important to determine how much time each relationship requires to maintain goodwill. A simple useful method is to list their time commitment as high, medium or low. If there's too many high maintenance people in your life, it may be time to scale back, or to unload some relationships that are predatory and one sided, draining you of time and resources.

People maintenance:
HIGH: Sandy   MEDIUM: Cindy, Marilyn, Brenda, Patty, Vanessa, Joel, Josie
LOW: Gary   AVOID: Maggie, Terry

What Is Life All About? The life has a purpose paradigm.

Once in a while, people ponder and ask what their purpose is in life… and the answer almost always eludes them. Perhaps there is no purpose except what we give ourselves. On a day to day basis, there are certain basic concerns and issues that tend to take up our time and attention. Here's the A to Z of creating a purpose for our lives, including: Obtaining free time from doing what other people expect you to do for them that does not benefit you.

Spending free time that feels good and fulfilling

a.   Self-improvement
b.   Self-expression
c.   Social contribution
d.   Entertainment
e.   Escapism
f.   Discovery
g.   Exploration

Increasing quality of free time

h.   Meaningful activities
i.   Interesting tasks
j.   Occupying boredom
k.   Improves financial stability
l.   Develops constructive relationships
m.   Results in advancing knowledge

Obtaining balance in personal life

n.   Finding one's niche in society
o.   Self-honesty
p.   Self-acceptance
q.   Self-respect
r.   Feeling at peace with oneself
s.   Feeling at peace with the world
t.   Overcoming fears and anxieties
u.   Accepting and embracing the future

Discovering universal truths and spiritual awareness

v.   Understanding physical laws of nature
w.   Understanding invisible laws of nature
x.   Understanding relationship principles of mankind
y.   Seeking and accepting God's will
z.   Fulfilling God's plan, if you believe

Let's discuss what these daily concerns entail:

Obtaining free time from doing what other people expect you to do for them that does not benefit you. The natural impulse of innocent children is selfishness and self-centeredness because that is a primordial primal survival instinct. As society's evolved, order and stability was impossible if everyone selfishly pursued their own egocentric goals without regards to the impact of their actions on others in society.

Eventually those egocentric children grow into adults and create unreasonable demands and expectations on others to do their bidding; therefore expanding their own egocentricity in an attempt to control others. Their childlike selfishness where their own actions to possess and hoard material things become perverse adult desires and activities to control the actions of others to exponentially expand their egocentric ability to hoard more by controlling the actions of others.

Family hierarchies and employers are particularly guilty of imposing unreasonable and unfair expectations on individuals, who if equity prevailed, would contribute proportionately to the amount of benefit they could expect in return for their selfless efforts to contribute to their families, organizations and society. Instead, social pressure and financial intimidation is utilized to force compliance by most people who desire to avoid conflict; and consequently, freedom and individualism is surrendered.

I only seek freedom to express my individualism, not as a mere naïve expression of childish egocentrism and selfishness, but to allow me the right to pursue those things and activities that I feel would bring personal satisfaction, fulfillment, meaning and happiness. As long as my intentions are good, and I do not trample on the rights of others, or my actions do not result in a detrimental effect on society, I should have a right to be me.

Spending free time that feels good and fulfilling. I want to have my life and times filled with positive and good feelings, where I don't imagine doing evil to those who hurt me or violate my human rights. I want to be free from fear and anxiety that evil people cause. I want to have fun and do things in safe environments where others are also happy, where I'm likely to make new friends and share good times.

a. Self-improvement in all areas of my life; physical, mental, emotional, financial and spiritual

    1) Physical health through improved nutrition, exercise, reduction in alcohol consumption.

    2) Mental health through schooling in interesting and practical subjects with income potential

    3) Emotional through establishing honest and mutually rewarding relationships

    4) Financial through prudent and persistent effort in promising fields and companies

    5) Spiritual through prayer, reflection, meditation and worshipping Father Jehovah God

b. Self-expression in everything that I do, without hesitation, self-consciousness, fear of embarrassment, or desire for validation, approval or admiration... 100% of the time.

c. Social contribution to better society and the lives of family, friends and my community, nation and the world whenever possible through charity and volunteerism.

d. Entertainment through both active and passive activities, including sports, movies, outdoors, partying, socializing, television, art, music and theatre.

e. Escapism through nature, prudent alcohol consumption, a little bit of Mary Jane, travel, nightclubs, strippers and sex.

f. Discovery of unknown, unexpected, unpredicted realities that broaden and deepen understanding of people, nature, the world, the universe, extra-sensory realities and God.

g. Exploration of internal and external realities and creating a bridge that connects, explains and unifies what is unified, and understanding what is discontinuous.

Increasing quality of free time is important because idle time can be the devil's workshop. As I earn free time from the reality of having to earn a survival, I want to ensure that my activities are worthwhile, as my time on earth is diminishing at an accelerated pace. I don't want to waste my remaining time on Earth doing stupid stuff like getting drunk and sleeping away my life.

h. Meaningful activities are plentiful, but motivation is weak due to laziness and low funds. Productive things to do include:

1) Inventing new products and bringing them to market

2) Writing books that create paradigm shifts in the global thinking of the elites

3) Producing singing and dancing videos for export to the world based on the music of my era

i. Interesting tasks keeps people engaged in activities where they can learn new skills, improve existing skills or feel satisfaction for doing something different or doing something well.

j. Occupying boredom is important to prevent depression, suicidal thoughts or just weird ideas that spontaneously surface from random disorganized introspection without an understanding and realistic perspective of prior events, whether real or imagined.

k. Improves financial stability because one of the worse situations people get stuck in beside poor health and rotten relationships is the lack of sufficient funds to make it to the end of the month, and insufficient savings, if any, to take care of those unforeseen emergency rainy days.

l.   Develops constructive relationships is a very difficult task because people don't really know who they are, what they want, why they should want what they think they want and so they tend to use others as tools to pursue their own self-interest, even though in the end run it turns out that their pursuits were not what they really should have gone after.

m.   Results in advancing knowledge is rarely a bad thing, unless of course a person wants to build a bomb to kill innocent people. Knowledge begets more knowledge and is the only thing that cost little to nothing in today's data filled cyberspace. It is possible to learn almost anything with an Internet connection… spend a day randomly browsing content on You Tube and Wikipedia, and suddenly the world opens up and it's amazing how diverse and profound knowledge is out there for the taking.

n.   Obtaining balance in personal life is important because focusing narrowly on a couple of areas limits one's worldview, exposure and appreciation for all that is available to learn, enjoy and share with others. Becoming well rounded, having multiple interests and areas of competency makes for a more interesting life.

o.   Finding one's niche in society is usually accomplished through careers, however, too often people lose their identity to their jobs and when asked who they are, they respond that they're a cop, or a teacher or a burger flipper, etc. That's not who they really are… that's what they do for a living for lack of something better to do that pays their monthly bills. People who do what they do because they have a passion for it, because it expresses inward values and feelings, a philosophy or moral beliefs come closest to discovering who they really are. All others are imposters.

p.   Self-honesty often evades people because their daily lives forces them to compromise their true feelings, opinions and behaviors to fit in to their work or social group norms. People find it difficult to admit that they are job prostitutes, who must bite their tongues and do what their bosses tell them to do, otherwise take a hike. People just can't handle the truth.

q.   Self-acceptance is essential for mental health, because even if everyone thinks you're wrong and despises you, but you still know who you are and you follow your own heart, then too bad on them because at the end of the day, it's you who you see in your mirror after washing your face.

r.   Self-respect goes beyond just acceptance. A person might accept that they are not too bright, or broke or whatever because their strategies in dealing with socioeconomic rules don't work very well. Self-respect says that even if you're considered a homeless beggar that you pride yourself at being the best damn beggar you can be.

s.   Feeling at peace with oneself goes hand in hand with self-acceptance and self-respect because it signifies a level of contentment, satisfaction and self-control though the world might be spinning around you, it does not sweep you up into chaos.

t.   Feeling at peace with the world is a difficult one because the diversity of values and all the evil things people do to each other is often too much to bear and all the bad news can sometimes feel overwhelming.

u. But if we allow ourselves to become depressed at the state of affairs over things that are beyond our control, how are we helping others or ourselves cope with reality? The world will take care of itself for better or for worse over the course of time, and it's highly unlikely anything that one individual does in their daily affairs will change the world in a day. Perhaps the most powerful people in the world can do that... maybe a captain onboard a nuclear submarine could change the world within minutes by launching a dozen nuclear tipped missiles. But changing the world for the better usually takes the efforts of many people working in concert toward a common vision, and it often takes a lifetime of hard work and sacrifices to change people's mindset.

v. Overcoming fears and anxieties from the childhood nightmares, insecurities, traumas, and feelings of neglect and danger is a lifelong task that is undertaken by adults who don't realize most of their emotional reactions and life views center around unresolved "boo boos" that they suffered as children. The greater the damage, the longer it takes to restore a sense of confidence, and unfortunately too many get to a point that they just stay conditioned to respond to uncertainties with more fear and anxiety.

w. Accepting and embracing the future is something most people find to be unsettling, so they feel compelled to make plans, goals and strategies to get from where they are to where they want to go. But unlike a trip itinerary, life is often totally unpredictable and the best laid plans of mice and men are often fumbled in the end zone with unintended consequences. Perhaps it's a less painful and wiser method to consider the possible options, to steer toward the preferred alternatives, but to expect the unexpected for better or for worse... then to deal with reality.

x. Discovering universal truths and spiritual awareness through understanding physical laws of nature is checking in with reality because anyone who thinks they can jump off the roof of a high rise building without a parachute should expect to die a sudden death... but the ride down can either be frightening or exhilarating.

y. Understanding invisible laws of nature is to admit that technology and science change over time, and what was once consider ridiculous or sci-fi usually end up becoming science fact. Just because something cannot be measured utilizing existing tools, doesn't make it an impossibility, otherwise men would have never stepped on the moon if people continued to believe that the world was flat.

z. Understanding relationship principles of mankind is essential to building positive and manageable relationships because Homo sapiens have genetically evolved with certain predispositions, among which are selfishness, violence, hatefulness, and deceit... but on the flip side; many have the propensity for kindness, love, and charity.

aa. Seeking and accepting God's will is an emotionally reassuring notion because it's likely everyone who has ever lived has endured some degree of pain and suffering... and it can be comforting to believe that a greater power of good is there to lift you back up every time. Fulfilling God's plan, if there is a real God with a customize plan.

Life in a Nutshell… observations from a parent to his children.

To my children…

I want to tell you that one of the few joys of my life have been you, my children. I know I've made a lot of mistakes in my life, and you've all been exposed to the consequences of my occasional poor behavior and bad decision-making. I've been very regretful and sorry that you've had to endure mental and emotional pain as a consequence of my unintentional mistakes. Some of the things I did were for self-gratification, without thinking of potential consequences on the ones who I loved. Other things I did out of frustration or unhappiness.

My life, as with most of humanity has been filled with much suffering and pain, both physically and emotionally. Life is a bitch, but if you're lucky and do the appropriate things at the right times, life can be a beach. I hope all of you will have better lives as the result of new wonderful opportunities that revolutionary technology will provide if mankind doesn't misuse it to wipe people out. I wish you will have lives filled with goodness, love, sense of purpose, spiritual awareness, and personal fulfillment. I've had that feeling on rare occasions, and it was very gratifying. I just wish that I had the capacity and fate to have felt fulfilled more often, and to have imparted more of that feeling to you.

Please be careful what you wish for, or what you say to your inner self. I once ridiculed life and old people by stating, "If I don't do all the things that I want to do by the time I'm 50, I'd rather die." In the world, there appears to be something called ironic justice and karma. Sometimes our wishes or fears help to design and bring about our own fate. Certainly life seems to give us what we really need in our hearts if are in it fully.

Before I die someday, I hope to have become happier with life. I've been happy with you, my children, but in my opinion, life on earth as it is sucks big time. Maybe it's because I've seen too much. Aside from my failure to become financially secure, I've met over 10,000 people during my life from a wide diversity (average meeting a new person every other day). What I've seen hasn't impressed me much. I hope you will have better experiences in your lives and pursuits. Money is important, but it isn't everything. But you already know that being without money is stressful and limits your freedom and happiness.

I feel the daily pains in my body from the process of growing older. Average life expectancy a hundred years ago was around 50 (for the poor even lower, and much higher for the wealthy), so I'm past the limit for a poor guy, were I alive a hundred years ago. But it's the new millennium, and people should be able to live to 100 or beyond in good health by mid-century. I've already told you my ideas for longevity... clone human bodies without heads, then transplant the old head with a new face onto the headless body. I have a lot of weird ideas because I'm usually ahead of the times, and most weird ideas someday become reality. So if you prepare to take advantage of weirdness, you can survive and profit. Unfortunately, it's easy to say, and I haven't become financially successful despite many attempts from Amway to insurance to real estate. Perhaps it hasn't been my fate. I'll admit to quitting before my time, and not trying hard enough.

Another problem I've had is with fear. For all the shit that I've had to go through in my life, I feel I've basically overcome most of my fears. I accept them, and then avoid the situations that cause me to feel fear. I haven't totally conquered them. When I say I've overcome them, I accept that I have them, and that it's likely I'll always have them to some extent. What have been my fears? Becoming imprisoned with evil people or not having much freedom or control over my day-to-day activities would really suck. I never want to go to jail again, not even overnight. I've always feared death, and can remember waking up from nightmares about war or earthquakes when I was a young boy between 5 and 8. Another problem is we often cause our fears to come true because our subconscious works on it to create a self-fulfilling prophecy.

Looking back, I don't feel much regret. I had many chances to have a financially stable life, having had good opportunities with Pacific Bell, Thrifty Drugs, CSU campuses, UCLA, Garfield Medical Center, and various insurance and real estate companies. I could be earning over $100,000 a year by now had I stuck with these jobs. But I just couldn't stand to do the same boring mundane tasks any longer. I guess a big part of success is just outlasting all the other people who quit early for one reason or another. Persistence pays off in the end run of the rat race.

I do wish I had the chance to take back several mistakes that cost me, such as breaking my foot, arguing with my bosses, womanizing, investing in time shares, and especially letting over consumption of alcohol get the best of me. But what ever happened already happened, and there's no way to take them back. Being sorry doesn't help, but learning my lessons from my stupid mistakes and changing my ways probably saved me from more grief... though there's always the unexpected.
If I had a way to do things all over again, I would certainly do things differently in at least half of my situations. I would have been a better father, a faithful husband, a sober citizen, and prayed a lot more than I did. Of course, if I had won the lotto, over 95 percent of my problems would be solved, but I'd probably assume many new problems that money can't solve, which I'm at a loss to guess what those problems could possibly be not having ever been financially secure in my entire life.

I guess I have to accept that I'm just another fool who has dreams of accomplishing great things, then stark reality showed me that I am just another mediocre man whose made plenty of mistakes, and just another soul who has come and will be gone from the face on the earth. There are at least a billion people who can do whatever I can do, and do it better than I. Whatever have been my small moments of slight achievements during my lifetime will blow away in the winds of time, with no consequence to the larger reality. I hope my life hasn't added much pain to yours. If it has, I sincerely apologize.

One day, as we look back and the dust scatters, so will memory of my life and time dissipate as it has for all who have preceded us. Try to learn how to recognize things you can control and those you can't. Live life, don't worry, be happy!

Seeking the Truth Paradigm – Essential Questions

Basic Question is to explain the reasons, outcomes and lessons from the following:
- What are your deepest heart-felt passions?
- What situations, ideas or people are worth dying for?
- What were the most "priceless" experiences in your life?
- What were the most expensive experiences in your life?
- What were the best deals in your life and the biggest rip offs?
- What were the most embarrassing moments in your life?
- What were the most dangerous and risky things you ever did?
- What were your highest accomplishments according to society's value system?
- What were your best achievements according to your own heart or values?
- What were the most selfless things you ever did for others?
- What were the most harmful and wrong things you ever did to yourself or others?
- If you could do it all over again, what events you would like to do over?
- What types of people (including race, sex, ethnicity, class, religion, education, occupation, socio-economic level, etc.) are you most comfortable being around?

On a scale of 1-10 (10 highest), what is your intrinsic emotional need for:

1. Validation, respect, and/or admiration from others
2. Help, assistance and charity from others
3. Sympathy or compassion from others
4. Monetary and material gain
5. Higher class status and titles (job, degrees, etc.)
6. Being seen around upper class people
7. Socially approved dress and appearance
8. Genuine love from those you care about
9. Attaining your highest innate potential
10. Peace of mind, freedom, and guiltless life
11. Moralize – feeling entitled to criticize and judge others
12. Entitlement – feeling you have intrinsic rights from society and others
13. Achievement – feeling the need to attain worthwhile goals
14. Learning – desire to gain greater knowledge through various avenues
15. Spirituality – desire to explain the unknown through religious dogma or its derivatives

What were the biggest lies you ever told? What types of living things have you ever killed (includes insects, plants, etc.). Do you believe in a soul and why do you need to feel that way? If you found convincing and irrefutable scientific evidence that the world as we know it will drastically and cataclysmically change in 3 years, how would you feel, how would you change your lifestyle and core beliefs/values and what if anything would you or could you do about it? In reflecting back on your life what people, events, and experiences made and still make life worth living?

Sometimes so much drama and pressures occur all at the same time, from work, family, spouses, parents, health, finances, government and what not, that life almost becomes unbearable and those occasional suicidal thoughts start to creep in. Then, another stronger competing voice hollers, "Don't sweat the small stuff... and it's all small stuff"... a line taken from a popular book with a similar title. I came up with an acronym, I D G A F 's that I applied to my day to day situations to put some levity and perspective into the small inconveniences and irritations in daily affairs and situations.

1. "I Don't Got A Friend"
2. "I Don't Gawk At Females"
3. "Investing Dandiest Greatest Achievements Frequently"
4. "Incident Damn Goof-up And F/Up"
5. "Ignorance Delivers Grief And Failure"
6. "Indifference Dumbfounds Grand Arrogant Fools"
7. "Intend doing great achievements frequently!"
8. "I Did Get A Feel"
9. "I Don't Get Any Fun"
10. "I Did Get Aromatic Flatulence"
11. "I done got another file"
12. "I Don't Get A Fish-dinner
13. "Inform Dumb Guy About F/ups"
14. "Intimidation Didn't Get A Fone
15. "Intimidation Didn't Get Assistant Fooled"
16. "I'll Do Guard Assessment Friday"
17. "Intend Doing Great Accurate Follow-up"
18. "I Don't Go After Fools"
19. "I Damn Go After Food!"
20. "I Don't Get Analysis Follow-up"
21. "In Doing Good And Finishing"
22. "I Don't Get A Fish-dinner".
23. "Inform Dumb Guy About F/ups"

24. "I'm Delightfully Gorgeous And Fine"
25. "I'm Dumb Giddish And Foolish"
26. "I Don't Give A Fuck"
27. "I Do Give A Fuck"
28. "I Do Get Anxiously Fearful"
29. "Initiative Doesn't Guarantee Achievement Frequency"
30. "I Don't Goof Around Frequently"
31. "I Do Get Aroused Frequently"
32. "I Do Get Around Fridays"
33. "I Do Get Achievements Frequently"
34. "Internalize Directions Go And Follow"
35. "I Don't Get Another Format"
36. "I Doodled Good And Frantically"
37. "Indefinite Delays Gets Ample Follow-ups"
38. "Initiative, Development, Goals, Action, Follow-through"
39. "I Do Get A Feeling"
40. "I Deliberately Go After Fulfillment"

The Population Boom Paradigm

World leaders and scientists grapple with the problem of
increasing global human population and its negative effects on the
ecosystem and depletion of natural resources, reduction in biodiversity,
geometric expansion of environmental pollution, global warming,
development leading to massive deforestation, and the rise in human
suffering due to insufficient regionalized food supplies. There has been
muffled talk among certain exclusive intellectual, scientific and political
groups to go beyond China's "one child" policy, and to utilize weaponized
diseases, new biotechnologies and nanotechnology not only to slow down
the human population growth rate, not merely to arrest the net population
growth, but instead to reduce global population by the end of this century
to less than 2 billion people.

The thought is somewhat based upon eugenics, and now made possible by advances in gene cluster sequencing, stem cell research and cloning technologies. In the not so distant future, there will be a push to usher in new criteria aimed at improving the evolutionary path of *Homo sapiens sapiens* from that of generally stupid, selfish, and uncreative followers to create a species of advanced self-actualized and self-motivated individuals who cooperate in concert to maintain the viability of Earth for its diverse life forms, including highly evolved human beings.

Some of the Darwinian thresholds that will define the new world human being may include:

Intelligence Parameters

Minimum I.Q. of 130 on Stanford-Binet Test or Cattrell of 140, and all of the following:
1.   Combined SAT of 1100, no score lower than 500 in either tests
2.   High School G.P.A. of 3.3 on 4.0 scale or 3.6 on 5.0 scale
3.   College G.P.A. of 3.0 on 4.0 scale
    4. Top 10 percentile score on at least one skill needed by global society: art, music, spatial, math, computer, speech, dance, game design, engineering, inventing, spiritual, or other practical aptitudes or skills.

Age and Health Parameters

Up to 70 years old, meeting the following criteria:
1.   MRI indicates no internal disease or damage to bones or organs
2.   DNA test indicates no genetic defects or predisposition to disease
3.   B.P. under 130/85 on empty stomach
4.   Body fat not to exceed 15%, and weight not to exceed 30% of Y2K body type standards

5. No STDs or history of dormant or incurable STD
6. No history of drug or alcohol abuse or convictions
7. No history of psychological or psychiatric problems
8. No history of violence
9. No functional disabilities (excepted as below)

All persons must meet the minimum benchmarks on an annual basis. Failure to pass benchmarks subjects individuals to a one year probationary period requiring monthly testing and evaluation. Failure to pass benchmarks after one year probation period subjects individual to euthanasia. Everyone over 70 is to be put to sleep.

Exception to 70 year old rule:
1. Individual possesses skills required for species advancement in science, art, technology, spirituality, philosophy, music, invention, engineering, computers, or other fundamental areas of knowledge deemed necessary for species survival.
2. Individual possesses monetary or convertible hard assets (discounting paper wealth such as stocks) exceeding 100 times the global average per capita income pegged to Y2K (estimated at $100,000 U.S.) adjusted for inflation. Immortality will be possible by the end of this century. Prior to discovery and manipulation of gene clusters that will enable immortality and the arrest of the aging process to maintain youthfulness, cloned bodies will become available for heads of those who can afford it.

Standards for eligibility for cloned bodies and cerebral transplantation:
1. Individuals who attain MENSA status (top 2% of population)

2. Individuals who perform physical tasks at top 5% of population, i.e. sports and stamina
3. Individuals possessing skills per age exception above
4. Individuals possessing assets per exception above
5. Individuals who are deemed "beautiful" by the global order

The Evolution of Man and Natural Selection Paradigm

Survival of the Fittest: based on DNA analyses, radio-carbon dating of archaeological evidence, and analyses of geological, paleontological, and botanical evidence of Homo sapiens lineage. While scientist theorize about the existence of a missing link, there is no scientific evidence to indicate that the ape and man evolved from the same parentage. However, the apparent biological continuum suggest that unicellular life became multicellular life, and simple life became more complex in adaptation to environmental pressures over long periods of time.

The newest race of evolved modern day humans is the Homo sapiens sapiens species, all of which derived from the first race of African Homo sapiens (Neatherthals, Homo-erectus, Co-magnum species became extinct).

Black race = 4-5 million years old
Yellow race = 1.5 million years old
White race = 1 million years old
Red race   = 20,000 years old
Brown race = 1,500 years old
Mixed races = 1,000 years old

The race that is the most adaptable and able to survive the greatest environmental changes survives the longest thus fits the definition of "survival of the fittest." Meteorological and topographic environment of each race accentuated the genetic development of various survival traits to enable its numbers to multiply.

How do culture, technology and political system affects human evolution. Major changes spell major opportunities. Those people who are able to recognize new and unexplored opportunities, who have the financial means or tenacity to pursue them will come out ahead. Most people will be unprepared for change, and will follow the prescribed paths that will become evident as political, financial, and religious leaders adjust to the changes. As usual, the common folks are the formless clay that will be molded into structure in the New World Order that will be the outcome of the impeding orchestrated global financial collapse.

Population growth and density continue to escalate as the sense of community rapidly depletes from greater societal distrust and alienation from its leaders, institutions, and neighbors. At least ten percent of the male populace have criminal records, are criminally inclined, or engage in illegal activities. Translated to terms of population demographics, 14,000,000 people are ex-felons, felons, and commit felonies in the United States. One percent of the people are nuts or in some state of mental disorder, like time bombs waiting to explode. That translates to over 3 million lunatics from sea to shining sea. Most are waiting for their 15 minutes of fame.

The New World Order Paradigm

In the year 2,020, cities will be engulfed in the flames of mass civil unrest and rioting as three-fourths of the populace will be out of work due to the planned manipulated crash of the stock market by the Secret World Government (the New World Order), and the failure of one-third of the world's financial computers due to the deliberate insider sabotage of the global financial network system with a false flag bug. All this will lead to seven years of tribulation and mass suffering, until the anti-Christ will appear to miraculously solved the world's problems and bring peace, prosperity, and order again. Then they will start to persecute Christians, and force anyone who wants to survive to take the "666" computer chip on their foreheads or hand.

100

The Black race took root in the original great continent, in the lush tropical zone where there was plenty of plant and animal life in Africa. As members of this race immigrated to other parts of the single continent its members adapted to the changing temperatures, topography, and available food and water supply. Eventually, the great continent separated along tectonic plates and created great oceans that caused the tribes to evolve as separate races, as adaptations to their immediate environments.

The Black race remained in the tropical zones in lush Africa and developed cultures that emphasized hunting the abundant game. The Yellow race adapted to the humid and wet climates of East Asia and developed farming and fishing. Much of the landmass that was home to the White race moved into colder regions, and they became lighter skin to adapt to the snow, which helped to conceal them for hunting. As there was less food and game living in colder regions, Whites evolved into a more aggressive species, as survival was more difficult in the harsher areas than colored races enjoyed in more temperate zones.

The Red race came by way of the Aleutian Islands and by seafarers from Asia, eventually settling the Americas, developing into the Native American tribes, the Aztecs, Incas, Mayans, and other "Indio" cultures. After the white man came to the "New World", the Brown race became a mixture of European and indigenous ancestry, as reflected in the mixed races of modern day Latin countries. The newest mixed race has become an increased trend due to more global mobility, which has placed different races in proximity to each other; consequently allowing a minority of its members to interbreed. The mixed race differentiates itself from the more homogenous races, as the gene pool reflected in the mixed race is markedly more dichotomous than in that of the older races.

Should nationalism, racism, and ethnocentric cultures wane as an outcome of the globalization of market-based economies due to practicalities, it is likely that over the next millennium (should mankind survive even another hundred years), baring authoritarian manipulation of the human gene pool, the youngest race of mixed genetic heritage will become the dominant and most advanced *Homo sapiens*. With the knowledge of the world's populations trends, there will continue to be great efforts by some in power to keep the White race "pure" through various cryptic and sinister means which include surreptitiously eliminating colored races through scientifically-engineered diseases that target the majority of non-white races, while leaving the white race minimally affected. Genetic genocide.

With the world's population growing geometrically, if unabated, the world population will be 30 billion by the year 2100. This is a number that would strain the world's food production capacity to its limit, not to mention the decrease in the amount of oxygen to breath and the amount of clean air and water. Pollution would become so great that the green house effect would accelerate the world's temperature increase along with such a great rise in sea level that all the major port cities in the world would become like the fabled city of Atlantis.

Consequently, the consortium of wealthy powerbrokers, financial elite, and descendants of the European kingdoms have been working to utilize scientific and technological advances to shape the future of humanity, the destiny of mankind in a New World Order. The goals and tactics of the New World Order groups (often referred to as the Tripartite Commission, Illuminate, or Commission on Foreign Relations, etc.) which are only the public and less secretive arms of the true world government are remarkably simple, and has been implemented since the mid 1950s and accelerated in the mid-1960s in response to cold-war nuclear Armageddon fears and paranoia. Nuclear bomb shelters were carved into granite mountains to house the elite classes of America, who were 99% white. The white Europeans and white Russians had similar contingency plans in place. If there could have been a way to save the elitist white classes in a world by confining them into nuclear bomb shelters for a five to ten years, then to return to the earth that was wiped clear of all other beings, without their progeny eventually becoming three legged and two headed species from the residual radiation contamination, they would have done it. The fact remains that the crude nuclear bombs of the past would have left the planet uninhabitable to any human race, animal, or most plants. Only the sea creatures could have remained as viable species on Earth.

In the mid-1960s, the military began to fund scientific research in manipulation of human DNA in an attempt to develop soldiers who could survive high dosages of radiation. They failed; however, much was learned about the genetic construction of human beings, and the racial differences were especially noted. Certain races tended to display various characteristic strengths and weaknesses that were more prevalent to one race than to another. For example, sickle cell anemia is far more prevalent in blacks than whites; lactose intolerance more prevalent in Asians than whites; alcoholism more prevalent in Native Americans than in whites; infertility more prevalent in whites than in other races. Blacks appeared to be more naturally gifted in athletics, Asians in math, Whites in invention, and Latinos in loyalty, as generalized examples.

Faced with the inevitable overpopulation of the earth, the Secret World Government formed a strategic plan to "trim the herds" and to attempt to selectively control population growth through various means, including:

1.   Development of various man-made diseases such as HIV/AIDS, utilizing retroviruses produced in the labs that are not normally found in nature. The method of infection would follow the basic needs of human beings for sex, water, and food.

2.   Development of various pharmaceuticals that while appearing to treat rather mild conditions actually create predisposition for future illnesses that may be brought on when the "key drugs" are later administered to trigger an onset of an eventual fatal outcome.

3.   Development of food additives which weaken the human immune system, and causes predisposition for various life threatening illnesses.

4.   Development of biological proteins that are added to shampoos, soap, cosmetics, and other hygienic products that can be absorbed, and assist in the weakening of the human immune system.

5.   Breeding more resilient and transferable diseases in livestock by feeding ground up livestock to cattle, pigs, and chickens.

6.   Encouraging poverty, homelessness, hopelessness, and inner city violence between disenfranchised racial groups.

7.   Permitting the proliferation of illegal drug use while pretending to hunt down the drug cartels. Drug dependency and addiction along with alcohol abuse and alcoholism usually leads into unprotected sex (increasing exposure to HIV), and violent crimes, such as assault, rape, and murder.

8.   Discourage the fraternization between heterosexuals to reduce the human reproductive rate. Encourage homosexuality as a method of birth control. While the various steps that are being taken to control population growth affect people of all races, the color races are disproportionately targeted and affected most by the different strategies listed above because their natural reproductive rates are four times that of whites.

The white race has become less fertile over the past hundred years, resulting in the rise of infertility clinics that are able to produce multiple births. Human cloning techniques are moving from the research labs to commercial applications and will eventually permit the Secret World Government to clone their progeny in their own image.   Usually, the man-made diseases, pharmaceuticals, and food additives can be identified by its surreptitious names, which are usually alpha numeric sequences that depict the chemical structure of the compounds utilized in its manufacturing or the basic nature of the disease components or etiology.

Finally all the pieces of the puzzle fit together. Science has caught up with eugenics fantasies. Gradually wipe out the colored races, except for certain groups with genetic traits that are beneficial to serve the Master White Race. Perfect multiple birthing and cloning techniques to repopulate the earth with enhanced genetically engineered white people according to the traits that are deemed necessary or desirable in the Brave New World Order. A goal of one billion whites and one billion colored people by the year 2100, instead of 30 billion could be possible. The next evolution of mankind could be by his own hands into super *Homo sapiens*.

Our little earth cannot handle 30 billion people within the next century. There will not be enough clean air to breath, clean   water to drink, and food to feed everyone; not ourselves, our parents and grandparents, our children, uncles and aunts, cousins, second-cousins, nieces, nephews, grandchildren and great-grandchildren yet to be. This is the dilemma that faces all nations and all people who share earth who will be chosen to propagate and survive as the human species after the year 2,100, and who has the right to choose the future progeny of the human race? What attributes will be determined to be beneficial for the race of mankind, and what genetic flaws must be erased in order for life on earth to continue unabated?

Since World War II, nations have already become economically polarized according to the notion of First, Second, and Third World status. The First tier is the western industrialized and technologically developed nations of Europe, North America, and Australia...the White world. The Second tier comprises the developing nations of Asia, the Middle-East, and Latin America. The Third tier describes the underdeveloped nations of Africa and Asia. While some economist might describe Japan as being a part of the First tier, in fact they are primarily a puppet of Anglo-European-American interests in Asia, and not full-fledged equal partners in the White world for no other reason than they are Yellow-skinned.

A diagram of the New World Order reflects the three economic and racial tiers generally accepted as today's reality.

THE EXISTING WORLD ORDER HEIRARCHICAL PARADIGM

TIER	NATIONS
1	U.S.A., U.K., ISRAEL, GERMANY, FRANCE, FINLAND
2	CANADA, SPAIN, ITALY, SWEDEN, W. EUROPE
3	JAPAN, CHINA, SO. KOREA, AUSTRALIA
4	RUSSIA, E. EUROPE, SE ASIA
5	MEXICO, MIDDLE-EAST, LATIN-AMERICA
6	AFRICA
7.	ARCTIC, ANTARCTIC

WORLD DOMINATION AND CONTROL

First Tier: U.S.A., U.K., GERMANY, FRANCE, W. EUROPE
Second Tier: CHINA, RUSSIA, JAPAN, SO. KOREA, W. EUROPE
Third Tier: CANADA, AUSTRALIA, E. EUROPE, SE ASIA

The USA, UK, Germany, France, and Western Europe are the top tier, who control modern technologies (the Chinese are independently advancing quickly in technology)

1. Military & space technology
2. Transportation vehicles manufacturing
   [planes, ships, automobiles, trains, etc.]
3. Food production & distribution
4. Computer technology & software
5. Medical-pharmaceutical research & technology
6. World-wide products distribution
7. Entertainment content

AUSTRALIA: Relocation of Rich & Famous Whites [abundant open space with low population]

JAPAN, CHINA, ASIA: Light manufacturing [abundant cheap labor]

MIDDLE-EAST: Oil production [abundant reserves]

MEXICO, LATIN-AMERICA: Tourism & illegal drugs [abundance
of poor people]

AFRICA: Natural resources [abundant unexplored resource, with
population dying off within the next century]

ARCTIC, ANTARCTIC: Scientific research [ecosystem sensitive]

DE FACTO RACIAL DEMOGRAPHICS IN NEW WORLD ORDER:

ALPHA – WHITE EUROPEANS/N.AMERICANS/AUSTRALIANS,
CANADIANS, RUSSIANS AND OTHER WHITE NATIONS

BETA – YELLOW ASIANS

DELTA – ARABS IN OIL RICH NATIONS

GAMMA – BROWN/RED PEOPLE IN MEXICO/S.AMERICA

EPSILON – BLACK AFRICANS

THE OLD WORLD ORDER PARADIGM

NATURAL DISASTER CYCLES

Massive natural environmental changes have occurred throughout
the eons, long before the advent of humans. These changes continue
today, and will undoubtedly continue after mankind is no longer a viable
species on planet earth. As with all natural phenomena, earth is in a
constant state of flux. Changing weather patterns, oceanic temperatures,
atmospheric composition, wind strength and direction, continental drift,
seabed accretion, fault stress, tidal patterns, flooding, drought, volcanic
eruptions, global warming, global cooling, topsoil erosion and depletion are
the normal cycles, and not the exception.

Human beings have been largely successful in adapting to the changing face of the earth due to technology, and to a great degree has been the architect of environmental change due to construction of cities where forests once flourished, creating lakes by damming rivers, and other superficial projects. Yet, humans are infants when it comes to affecting natural phenomenon, and are ill equipped to stop natural disasters. No building has ever been built that can not be toppled by a super earthquake. Few homes exist that can survive a Level 5 tornado or hurricane head-on. With the exception of large dams, no structures exist that can hold back torrential rain and flooding. And no defensive system has ever been built that can shoot a meteor, asteroid, or comet out of the heavens before it hits the earth. Humans are fragile surface dwellers in a constantly changing hostile world.

THE CYCLICAL NATURE OF THE UNIVERSE PARADIGM

The normal three physical states of water demonstrate the cyclical nature of things on earth. The total amount of water remains static, it changes state from ice to liquid to gas, depending on the amount of energy applied to its molecules. The basic building block and basic shape of things is spherical, from subatomic particles to stars, indicating a uniform principle in the physical universe. Presuming natural laws may be universally applied on earth as in other places in the universe, a plausible scenario can be made to explain theological thought to scientific evidence.

Garden of Eden was on Mars: face on mars are pyramids Adam & Eve sent to earth: life began as Neanderthals seeds from Martian life fell on earth from passing of planet X that took away atmosphere, water, and life form and deposited on earth. God created all creatures on earth. Life evolved on planets that at some point supported water and an atmosphere on Venus, Mars, and Earth that also held abundant "building block" chemicals and "Goldie Lock" temperature range needed for some forms of life.

Periodically, Earth's internal heat becomes too great and escapes through deep ocean floor vents, and results in tremendous earthquakes and volcanoes that darken the sky to create an ice age. The civilization that created the pyramids on Mars, the sphinx, and the pyramids on earth (Mayan, Egyptian, etc.) are descendents of original "Adam & Eve"... traces of their civilization are left after it is bounced back to the primeval ages after each cyclical earth cleansing ice age. The "immortals" have been trying to find the right balance between science & technology and the development of primal human emotions and instincts in a race to liberate humans from the limitations of the Earth's cleansing cycle of destruction and rebirth. But until humans can unite and become a peaceful race, other "angels" or immortals will not give mankind the secrets to escape the endless terrene cycle of periodic destruction.

Periodically, Planet X or Nibiru that orbits its infrared dwaft star comprises the missing mass from our solar system passes through our solar system and causes cataclysmic changes on many planets, including the Earth. As the huge Planet X passes it's enormous gravity creates mountains from seabed, takes away atmosphere, pulls up oceans that later falls back as constant rain, deposits moons from other worlds, creates a period of prolong meteor and asteroid activity and bombardment of planets and moons, takes material from one planet and deposits traces on other planets as it passes, etc.

Every 1,000 - 10,000 years, asteroids, comets, and large meteors strike the earth like bullets traveling 30,000 to 100,000 mph or more, causing cataclysmic effects on the ecosystem and destroying most forms of life. Life then evolves again according to adaptation and survival of the fittest. Every 100 to 1,000 years, new incurable diseases ravage the earth, killing various species in great numbers, leaving those that survive and adapt to propagate, including human beings.

UNNATURAL – ARTIFICIAL SELECTION PARADIGM

Conspiracy theories abound regarding all types of unsolved matters whether it be the assassination of Dr. Martin Luther King, JFK, Robert Kennedy, UFOs, pyramids on Mars, Hubble Telescope images, or even the alleged closet affairs of President Bill Clinton. A recurring theory exists that connects the assassination of JFK (President John F. Kennedy), AIDS, biological weapons of genocide, Africa, the Federal Reserve and the world's secret government. Back in 1963, during the height of the cold war with Russia, one of the "black projects" of the military was to develop a biological weapon, a disease that could wipe out the enemy; the communists (Cubans, Russians, North Koreans, North Vietnamese, and Red Chinese, etc.).

President John Kennedy had many enemies, including the Russians, the exiled Cubans for the Bay of Pigs fiasco, Fidel Castro, the Mafia for Attorney General Robert Kennedy's crack down on organized crime (the Kennedy's were the sons of Joseph Kennedy, of a competing Irish crime syndicate), J. Edgar Hoover, the closet gay FBI Director who detested the President's womanizing with Marilyn Monroe and other glamorous women, and white supremacists who detested his support of the rights of Negroes (African-Americans).

During this era, the effort to develop a biological weapon of mass destruction that would attack only the enemy was proposed that would kill only specific ethnicities, while not harming friendly groups. This type of thinking was behind efforts to infect cows milk that seemed to debilitate Asians more than whites; consequently, it was discovered that 80 percent of Asians are allergic to cow's milk, as they are generally lactose intolerant.

The first step was to create a new virus that could not easily be identified, thus traced back to or blamed on the military. Any type of genocidal weapon would further infuriate Americans, due to the horrors the world experienced during World War II, when Adolph Hitler attempted to exterminate all persons of Jewish ancestry. Ex-Nazi scientists and medical researchers who had done genocidal experiments on the Jews led the search for this new weapon of mass destruction. A bovine immunodeficiency virus was noted as one that killed only cows, but was not passed to humans via cow's milk. It was also noted that a certain venereal disease found in sheep was easily passed to humans. Experiments at the DNA level were done to genetically engineer a virus that could pass from the cow to the sheep. They were successful. Bovine immuno-deficiency virus was transformed into a sheep immunodeficiency virus that was only one step from being transmittable to humans.

They needed a test population that was not advanced enough to know what had hit them. And they needed societies that interacted under conditions that were conducive to diseases, exhibited close social and family ties, and had minimal mobility. African tribal societies during the 1960s and 1970s exhibited all of these desired laboratory requirements. But it was discovered that the new genetically engineered virus was not restricted to any human ethnicity due to the complex mixture in the human gene pool. The new retrovirus could infect almost all humans. The secret world government was eventually briefed about the results of these retrovirus experiments, and decided that the virus should be tested on Africans for several reasons.

First, Africans were technologically backwards. They were close-knit, tribal, sexually prolific, and lived under conditions that were conducive to new diseases. The world community would not have any hint that an apparent new disease was man-made. The problem remained that the sheep as host was not indigenous to Africa.

So clever government scientists took the monkey, and engineered a virus that could be transmittable from monkeys to humans. One very interesting aspect of man-made retroviruses is that it is very species-specific. That means if the virus was based to affect the DNA of a sheep, it will not affect monkeys. And if a virus was made to affect a particular type of monkey, it won't affect gorillas or baboons. The virus that was engineered was based on particular similarities found in the DNA of the human and the jungle tree monkey that is typically used in medical research. That's why gorillas don't contract AIDS; only humans and medical research tree monkeys.

The secret white world government wanted to kill Africans for several reasons; to rid the world of what they considered to be genetically inferior blacks (actually they fear blacks because In general blacks are physically superior, more creative, talented, and as or more intelligent than whites); to clear resistance to the economic take over of the richest continent on planet earth, Africa; and to do it in a way that the conspiracy would not be evident because world opinion was against colonialism. Colonialism could not apply if all the population were eliminated.

President Kennedy eventually found out about this plot, and he objected strongly and ordered the project to be stopped. He even confessed his abhorrence to this genocidal plot to his mistress, Marilyn Monroe (this was in addition to his plan to abolish the Federal Reserve Bank that got him in trouble). Consequently, they both had to be eliminated to protect the secret government's conspiracy. Now, with Kennedy out of the way, the work continued to test the virus on Africans. The virus was introduced to laboratory monkeys, who were then let out into the African jungles to interbreed. But the transfer of the virus by monkey bites to humans was rare, at best sporadic, and usually occurred to children, who did not have sex, thus could not transfer the disease easily. After ten years, a decision was made to speed up the process. During the mid-70s, the United Nation's World Health Organization (WHO) was used as an unsuspecting agent in transferring the AIDS virus via the smallpox vaccine to millions of Africans. Over the next 5-10 years, the Africans became part of a living experimental disease laboratory.

J. Edgar Hoover, who knew of the plans to assassinate J.F.K. had a hatred of homosexuals because he was a closet gay, who could not fulfill his fantasies. During the early 1980's, Edgar Hoover authorized the engineering of a hepatitis epidemic among the gay population in San Francisco, when the AIDS virus that was now infecting upwards to 50 percent of the blood imported from Africa via Haiti (America's cheap blood supply), was used to make gamma-globulin and other blood products used to combat the hepatitis outbreak. The rest is history, as the disease passed from Africans and Haitians to homosexuals to heterosexuals, and affecting hemophiliacs and intravenous drug users. If we look at the rate of infection of Africans (upwards to 60 percent in some tribes), extrapolate backwards to the likely period of the earlier infections, it would be evident that it coincided with the UN's smallpox vaccination program, and not to any particular monkey bite.

And it would be evident that AIDS was present in Africa ten years before the hepatitis outbreak among American homosexual men. Without a cure, even with the high proclivity for procreation, at the present rate of infection, Africans will almost become extinct within another century, and the riches of Africa will be up for grabs by the white race who comprise over 90% of the world's elite, wealthy and powerful.

THE CURRENT WORLD ORDER PARADIGM

Money is used by governments toward political ends, to prop up puppet or sympathetic governments, or to bribe political and government officials to tow the line. Government raises money through involuntary servitude... taxes and penalty assessments for non-conformity... fines. Government represents itself as the protector of the public interest and directs most of its funds to that service; however, since the greatest amounts of money are involved...favoritism, embezzlement, bribery, and kickbacks occur at any given time somewhere in the system of things.

Money is used by corporations to bribe government officials to obtain favorable legislation or regulations. Mega global corporations raise money by mass marketing of products that they manufacture and distribute with the least amount of labor and raw materials, with the maximum amount of price inflation according to a market demand that they attempt to create by clever and quasi-deceptive mass marketing and packaging techniques that play on the emotional needs of potential consumers according to their marketing propensities which are based on cultural, ethnic, gender, religious, political, age, educational, income, and interest demographics, etc. Most corporations represent itself as the provider for the public needs, delivering products and services that are needed or desired by the public.

Money is used by criminal organizations to bribe or intimidate public officials into overlooking crime and redirecting law enforcement efforts to other criminal segments. Criminal organizations raise money by use of violence to create an environment of fear so they may market products that are cater to human vices, or to defraud the innocent public. Criminal organizations represent itself as providing for entertainment needs of a large segment of the public appetite for illegal sex, drugs, gambling, and other vices. Confusion occur when government permits and legitimizes activities that have always been traditional criminal domain, such as gambling, by permitting and sometimes collusion with criminal elements in card clubs and casinos. Lottery and bingo are legitimized gambling operations.

Confusion occur when corporations encourage investments in activities that have traditionally been criminal domain, such as gambling by developing mega gambling casinos, glamorizing and selling sex on cinema, and exposing our children to it, as if it were okay, thus conditioning future acceptance and participation. The stock market, while euphemistically called investing, is actually gambling, and the odds for winning in the long run may not be any better than playing blackjacks.

Confusion occur when criminal elements support various local causes supported by politicians, wine and dine bankers and public officials, and judges, etc. while appearing to the public to be legitimate, but known to the young and street level masses as being criminal. The ability of organized criminals to amass great sums of capital creates the perception that it's just another business. The reality is that the top echelons of all three segments of society bear great similarities... all feel a certain degree of immunity from the law due to "connections" and the ability to buy "legal protection", to be able to hire investigators and "enforcers" to protect their interest.

Government uses law enforcement and the military that blindly carry out actions against the public that may or may not be the result of rational or "good" laws. When individuals or groups challenge or threaten the political and economic interests of the status quo government, its thugs are used to rein in the "troublemakers", to discredit them in the public eye, to imprison them, and if all peaceful means fail, to assassinate them. Corporate executives hire bodyguards and soldiers of fortune, mercenaries who conduct covert missions against perceived dangerous competitors. If smaller competitors are able to hurt their profits, then various tactics may be employed to
remedy the "problem", including bribery, hiring their key executives, management and/or technical talents, and if all fails, burn down a hotel such as the Raddisson at their competitors annual business meeting, and blame it on some homeless alcoholic homosexual. Criminal elements utilize prostitutes and hit men to set up their targets, to make them vulnerable to public humiliation or fearful of violent retribution against them and/or their families and businesses.

All three groups are organized as the primary exploiters of public trust, who manipulate the financial structure of capitalistic societies. These groups primarily have dominion over their particular fields of interests, however will compete against each other in segments where their activities overlap, and they often fight ferocious over the turf, which is competing for customers. For example, in the temporal nature of money, crime and punishment, a $1 million crime deserves greater punishment time because it would take more time to accrue $1 million than let's say $1,000, and more likely, more people are hurt by larger monetary losses than by lesser losses. But when large corporations violate laws that put the public at risk, threaten to collapse the economy or through fraudulent financial products cause the ruination of millions of hard working citizens, they usually get a slap on the hands with a relatively paltry fine and no jail time. The government keeps the fines and individuals must resort to expensive private legal actions against the corporate robber barons who conveniently use government protection by declaring bankruptcy. The law permits individuals to declare bankruptcy only once every ten years, but corporations can do it over and over again, simply by changing their names or reincorporating as another entity.

ENVIRONMENTAL POLLUTION PARADIGM

There exist natural and man-made pollution. Natural pollution includes lightning caused wildfires, excrements from animals such as cows, which appear to have deleterious affects on the upper atmosphere's ozone layer, and droughts, which cause
massive loss of top soil. Man-made pollution comes from industrial and metropolitan wastes generated by explosive population growth that causes exponential increases in the demand for manufactured products.

Pollution occurs at every level; at the mineral extraction site; at the manufacturing site; and at the consumption site. Chemicals are utilized in various processes which have toxic affects on living things, such as fish, fowl, plants, mammals, and humans. Manufactured products do not decay back to base elements, as do organic wastes; consequently, both land and water become contaminated with non-biodegradable wastes for very long durations. Man-made pollution from cities and industries dump billions of tons of toxic chemical wastes that pollute water, air, and soil, rendering the habitat unsafe for future generations.

The accumulation of wastes, toxic chemicals, and other pollutants continue to expand in geometric proportions as the onward march for technological progress and financial gains blind people to the fact that the earth is a limited biosphere on the brink of overpopulation and over pollution. The human species has a choice to reduce environmental pollution, adapt to more prevalent pollutants, or eventually to become an endangered, or extinct species. Adapting to an increasingly toxic environment would most likely entail the protection of the elite classes of wealthy powerbrokers, possibly in dome communities, while commoners will continue to suffer in the open unprotected environment.

Industrialized nations have only recently in the past two decades began to legislate more effective restrictions against industrial pollution; however, the explosive growth of cities has created monumental trash dumps that tower into the sky. Developing nations have rarely dealt with increasing environmental damage, as their short term economic and monetary interests have priority over any long-term environmental pollution strategy.

New biotechnologies that utilize bacteria to break down various forms of chemical pollutants is still an infant industry, and effective but safe products won't be available on a large scale for another decade. Long-term cellular DNA damage to fetuses and children resulting from environmental pollution manifests as cancer and other diseases in adulthood that decrease the quality of health and lifespan. Due to the fact that rivers, air, and underground aquifers do not respect national boundaries, pollution from any one nation usually affects the ecology of its neighbors. Until all of the nations of the world unite and work together to reduce pollution, the lives of all human beings are threaten.

OVERPOPULATION PARADIGM

How many people can mother earth support? As the population has exploded from 1 billion to almost 6 billion in less than one century, it is projected at the present rate, the planet will be drowning in 30 billion people within the next century. But long before that time, there will be pandemic deaths from incurable diseases; mass starvation from crop failures caused by hostile weather; great wars between many nations fighting over land, religion, or greed; reduced life span due to poverty and environmental pollution; and massive lost of life from natural and nuclear catastrophes.

In nature, only those species that can adapt to changes in the environment continue to survive. Human beings are still bounded by that fact. In nature, when the numbers of certain species become too large to be fed and supported by the natural environment, famine, disease, and starvation kills a great number, thereby trimming the herds and flocks to that which can co-exist in the limited environment. When the human population exceeds the limits of the environment to nourish such life, massive famine, disease, and starvation will trim the herds and flocks in the cities and megalopolises. Perhaps governments will fall, anarchy will reign for a time, then a new cycle of order will be restored as the reduced population becomes manageable again.

Perhaps human beings are doomed to become extinct on this planet until such time as the earth is given time to heal itself. The survival of the fittest will be those human beings whose progeny are able to survive in a polluted world, and those who are able to escape by space travel to other life supporting planets. But the most probably scenario is for humans to die in great numbers long before mankind figures out a way to travel to a hospitable substitute planet, where base human impulses will begin the same destructive behavior on distant worlds.

Perhaps human beings can someday overcome their natural urge to pollute, destroy, and alter their environment. Perhaps someday far more enlightened leadership shall prevail over the masses of lost, spoiled, and apathetic human beings, and save our world. Technology, like most human advances, continues to change people's daily lives in very pervasive ways. However, technology is not the panacea for all human problems, and in fact, often acts to create new problems, such as massive underemployment. In many instances, depending upon the tasks to be performed, a live interactive human being is more efficient or cost-effective than robots, machines, computers, and various technologies. All machines need to be serviced, otherwise they break down with wear and tear. They are not completely tireless. They overheat, blow fuses, short out, grind out gears and bearing, need oil changes, and parts need to be replaced. That means downtime and inefficiency.

It is not possible for present day machines to be maintained and serviced without human beings. High-tech demands high investment of capital. Even with relatively minor changes that humans can immediately adapt to, computer software would need to be rewritten, machines would need to be reset, and in many cases completely redesigned and refashioned by humans.

The great fear of massive socio-economic breakdown at the end of the millennium perpetrated by shortsighted computer programs that fail to differentiate between 1900 and 2000 turned out to be inconsequential. However, the ability of criminals to hack into systems to steal confidential data whether from individuals, corporations, ISPs or data servers will cast a dark shadow on people's trust in future technology and the proposed cashless societies.

Corporations are discovering that it is often less expensive and more efficient to employ people to do the work that was once earmarked for high tech robots and computers. It would take a far stretch of the imagination to visualize a world where machines would do everything for humans. If for no other reason, people need people, as we are social animals most of the time. For most parts, humans are still the most efficient machine ever created, operating for hours for the price of a few hamburgers. But, technology is here to stay as sure as the change from riding horses to driving automobiles.

How can mankind undiscover fire? Despite limitations that are peculiar to either machines and/or people, some exciting technological discoveries are on the horizon that can be of great benefit to humanity. Humans are within a decade of producing automotive engines that run on electrolysis of water, diseases that can be cured by irradiation with Pico waves (that kill viruses including AIDS), flying via positron emissions and electromagnetic repulsion, deep space travel via high intensity controlled negatron bursts, supersonic flying cars, thought-projection amplification, skin and hair regeneration, non-organic food substitutes, and encapsulated nutritional concentrates for enhancing physical, emotional, mental, or sexual performance.

A humanistic life supplemented by technological progress that solves the problems of human societies, rather than adding to the destruction of the earth, would be a noble and necessary goal for technology. We don't need another weapon system that is capable of destroying all life on our planet, with the exception of planetary defense against rogue comets or invasion by advanced ETs. We don't need to quicken the "1984" and "Brave New World" scenarios just because super computers, microelectronics, and public paranoia permits it.

We are like roaches, scurrying for scraps of food in our effort to stay alive. Warfare appears to have been a method of natural selection and population control to counter-balance the prolific tendency of human beings to overpopulate the earth, thus becoming an ecological threat to the ecosphere, the balance of nature. On the surface it would appear that war is a manmade phenomena, but studies of animal societies and insect communities indicate that overpopulation leads to massive aggression and warfare.

Humans may be playing out the process of natural selection, but people think they are in control of the process. If humans are in control of this aspect of natural selection, then why can't we turn wars on and off at will? Why does it almost always entail great casualties, before human societies resolve their differences, when the stronger conquers the weaker through massive wars of destruction or attrition? The worldwide scale wars like the Napoleonic, WWI, WWII, Hundred Years War, Roman and Trojan Wars, and the Crusades had a real effect of trimming back the population of their time. Were we to experience WWIII, a nuclear holocaust will place the human species on the brink of extinction. Those who might survive would produce a mutant progeny, thus new species would occur as result of natural selection, survival of the fittest.

Most humans who subscribe to religious thought believe that death is only the end of our physical existence, that our souls continue, remaining alive in spirit form, until such time as it is given eternal life or destroyed by God at the end of time as we know it. At the end of physical time, the temporal nature of our existence ceases to affect our souls, as the soul's immortality renders linear time inapplicable. Or, perhaps there is no life after death, and our perception of reality, presence, or even dreaming ceases upon physical death. Perhaps there is only life or death; existence, or non-existence. We can only surmise, as not one soul has come back to prove the existence of a previous or future lives.

Due to the vastness of controversial differences that abound in this nation, the most heterogeneous society in the history of mankind, there exist an undercurrent of conflict and hatred among its residents based on differences inherent to group identification. If the American experiment fails, then perhaps the future of mankind will rekindle the homogenous warring nation states era of history. And in an age that is already proliferated with nuclear weapons, it would not take but a few zealots and terrorists to touch off the beginning of the end. So it has become even more increasing essential to the survival of mankind that America must recover its confidence and resolve to be a successful example and leader of social, political, and economic democracy. America must prove that the strength of American ideals enables people from all races, ethnicities, cultures, religions, and gender to share in a fair and lasting prosperity. If America sheds its commitment to individual freedom and progress, then the world is doomed to embrace authoritarian rulers with false promises of hope. Hitler was very successful in playing on the hopes and anger of the downtrodden, and we are seeing a strong resurgence of Neo-Nazi sentiments today.

ECONOMIC DISPARITY PARADIGM

America is being raped by the corporate greed of the international pirates that include the leadership of the largest multi-national American, European, and Japanese   conglomerates. American executives now earn an average more than 100 times the wages of the average worker, during a time of massive lay-offs due to corporate downsizing, and personal bankruptcies. The global community is regressing to a stage of feudal nation-states, where the economic disparity between the ruling classes and the masses once again becomes legitimized by its institutions, where the rich minority exercises domination over the majority poor, and the primary purpose of the consumer classes is to provide a vehicle of profit for the wealthy equity holders.

Despite so-called experts who perpetually disagree with each other, the economy can be explained in rather simple terms and concepts. There are four basic components of any economy; first, natural resources; second, manmade goods and services; third, distribution; and finally, value that is created by demand. When any of these economic elements become unbalanced, the economy skews toward those who controls any of its elements. When any particular group controls the first three components, they develop a virtual monopoly on the fourth.

Different political systems utilize laws to alter the natural relationship between these four elements of economy to shift wealth from its unprotected classes (the poor and consumer classes) to its protected classes (economically and politically powerful). If left alone, without governmental restrictions, except that transactions should be based on a doctrine of mutually fair exchange of similar value (of whatever equivalent method of trade), economic systems would naturally tend to become balanced systems. If you don't believe it, name one person who you know who would knowingly consent to a barter situation where his own interests becomes secondary to making a profit for the other guy. If so, let's just give away the store. But in reality, with the legitimization and collusion of special interest government, the economic interests of the average citizen is subrogated to the self-perpetuating interests of the power brokers who attend to the economic interests of the ruling class, and depend on special interest support to maintain their positions.

Institutionalized inequities are more apparent in certain industries than in others; however it pervades the entire economic structure of America, and is legitimized by government, and is taught in universities, as the way things should be, further perpetuating a system that primarily serves the will of the wealthy. The real causes of economic recession are the imbalances that are created when vast sums of money leaves the country from an imbalance of trade, the exporting of American jobs by both American and internationally-owned companies, and the uncontrolled runaway debt incurred at all levels of the economy, from individual to corporate and government.

Presently, the total net worth of all the property in America has been estimated at $70 trillion (not including exaggerated stock market portfolio values). The gross productivity of the economy (GDP) is approximately $15 trillion per year, and the federal budget about one-fourth of the GDP as the national deficit continues to swell to equal the GDP. Federal, state, and local taxes and user fees now account for about 40% of the average household's expenses. The top 1% of the population owns one-half of all the wealth in America (the top 5% owns almost three-fourth), the bottom fourth owns less than 1% of America, and the middle-class owns the balance (24%). America is rapidly becoming a two-class society, of the rich versus the poor. Mankind's history is filled with examples of civilizations whose governments were eventually toppled by the poor after the disparity between rich and poor become obscene and inhumane.

THE STOCKMARKET GAMBLE PARADIGM

A baffling contradiction appears in our economy today, where the stock market posts record highs, breaking the 14000 barrier while underemployment is at a record high. Why at a time of great stockholder profits are a record number of individuals going bankrupt as millions are losing their jobs? Where is all the money going? Why are the profits not being reinvested into companies to maintain jobs?

Are the wealthy, armed with inside boardroom information, taking advantage of institutional investors such as public pension plans, leaving them to hold the bag? Taken as a group, investment experts are no more effective in predicting the future value of stocks than flipping a coin or throwing darts blind-folded. The real money is being made by those with the inside track, friends of corporate management who are leaked insider information, and can make clever buy and sell decisions that are subsequently mimicked by the public sector institutional investors and John Q. Public. The lag in time between insider trading and the movement of large blocks of public sector stock equals big profits for the clever private investors who are able to buy low and sell high.

WORKERS' RIGHTS PARADIGM

The typical American worker has lately been characterized as being lazy and illiterate. Americans work a shorter average work week than the Japanese. So what? Before collective bargaining, corporate abuse of the American worker was severe. Twelve to sixteen hour days and six day work weeks were common. Forced child labor was a disgrace. Working conditions were hazardous and contemptible. Workers finally exerted their collective voice for humane treatment, resulting in the rise of unions and protective legislation.

Much of America's economic growth occurred during a period of massive unionization. With the gradual demise of union influence (due in part to unions taking on the similar insensitive attitudes as traditional management, corruption, and lackluster gains for its employees) during a period characterized by more responsible employee protection regulations, we have seen a corresponding decrease in worker productivity. When unions were active, workers felt a sense of banning together for common purposes, to demand fairness from management. The sense of camaraderie created a pride that translated to a reputation for hard work and quality products.

Widespread employee rights legislation took the thunder out of the union movement. Why should workers pay union dues to obtain the same benefits and wage increases that would be provided by employers without bargaining units? After President Reagan fired all of the air traffic controllers who were on a union strike (and banned them from future federal jobs), the public realized how ineffectual unions could be. Unionized workers who struck the Los Angeles Herald-Examiner newspaper never received a raise, nor got their jobs back. Instead, the paper eventually went out of business. These absolute attitudes of non-compromise and disregard for unionized worker rights by government and big business sent a strong message to the American worker; if you strike, take a hike.

The American worker was steadily becoming demoralized. Job security was no longer a viable concept. It would not be uncommon for workers to experience unpredictable and periodic lay-offs when various sectors of the economy would experience recessions as a result of political, corporate, and international manipulations.

Technology is quickly changing the face of the American work place, realigning the biological clock to the pace of computerized mechanisms of work in the office and assembly lines. The workplace was becoming a dehumanizing experience. It become unlawful to express personal opinions, and the exercise of the freedom of speech often resulted in punitive sanctions by the employer or governmental agencies. Workers not only had to worry about job security as a function of economic factors, but had to be concerned about the idle things they said at the workplace that might be interpreted by people as being sexist, racist, or anti-gay. Interpersonal relations had to suffer as a people became reticent to expose their true feelings. While restraint may have had a superficial effect of smoothing over relations at work, a deep undercurrent of estrangement, alienation, and demoralization of the American worker developed, often leading to greater long-term stress-related problems. Worker dissatisfaction statistically translates to increased absenteeism caused by on-the-job injuries, illnesses, and personal leaves; consequently a decrease in productivity. To make matters worse, executive compensation was often at the expense of worker layoffs. Let the workers eat cake or worse.

An attitude of "let the workers be damned", and blame the workers for bad management decisions did little to focus attention on the real causes of America's economic problems... corporate greed, decreased reinvestment in the means of
production, overextended credit debts, exportation of American jobs, control of economic factors by a minority of the multi-national wealthy elite, and politicians who feel more responsive to special interests than to the electorate. The American worker built this great nation. When the American worker is healthy, the nation's economy is healthy. When the American worker cannot earn enough to be the mass consumers of the products of the industries where they are employed, then the economy will suffer. If corporations cannot sell their goods, then they too will suffer.

Economics is cyclical. Each dollar earned by a typical worker is recycled in the internal economy 7 to 10 times, creating additional jobs and economic opportunities. American's have a rich tradition of being resourceful, and the vast majority of new jobs since 1970 have been created by small businesses during the same period when most major corporations have laid off millions of workers as part of downsizing strategies to
increase corporate profits and executive compensation.

The wealthy powerbrokers are sowing the seeds for worker rebellion. Corporate executives must realize that in the long run, the prosperity of their companies is directly proportional to the prosperity of their workers. The American worker can become a formidable foe to corporate interests when pressed to the wall. Corporate America has been able to obtain pro-business special interest tax breaks and legislation only because the average voter has been relatively satisfied, apathetic and disinterested in political action.

A dissatisfied electorate can become a formidable foe to politicians who they believe have lead to their economic misfortunes; and consequently, could elect a new breed of responsible politicians who would be more responsive to worker interests. Only shortsighted corporate executives would fail to recognize that keeping the American worker happy is good for business and long-term corporate health. Unfortunately, American corporations appear to be suffering from acute executive myopia.

A redistribution of wealth from the rich to the poor, socialism, returning to a basic barter system, or any revolutionary change in the economy is not suggested. Positive changes should be developed in prudent, predictable, and incremental steps to minimize the systemic shock that invariably results in great suffering for the vast majority of people (just look at what instant change has done to cripple the former Soviet Union). We should not dismantle all the positive institutions and systems that exist, but instead improve and encourage the development of a more motivated, productive, and wealthy middle class to ensure a diverse economic foundation that can survive in the global economic markets.

Strengthening the middle class creates consistent markets for more products and services while providing the wealthy class greater opportunities to amass even greater fortunes. The larger tax base enables government to provide needed infrastructure improvements, funds to reduce the federal debt, support of social, national defense, and technological advancement expenditures. The shrinking middle-class can have a devastating effect on the economic survival of our nation, and decreases opportunities for both domestic and international businesses. While many cash fluid rich can increase net worth a hundred folds during a recession or depression by their ability to buy depressed property at highly discounted prices from people who are cash starved, the long-term devastation of a recession or depression actually decreases the amassing of fortunes when compared to performance possible during economic boom periods.

REAL VS. ARTIFICIAL VALUE

The real things of value to life on earth are usually taken for granted while artificial value is inferred to manmade things that have little intrinsic value other than social prestige, diversion, or entertainment. Take for instance water, without which life as we know it could not exist. People assume there will always be water to sustain life, then proceed to poison the very life giving resource of which there is a limited supply in the closed ecosystem known as Earth. Water and the action of the waves can be harnessed to drive electrical turbines, hydrolyzed to produce hydrogen and oxygen, or to irrigate crops that contribute back to the ecosystem. Yet water as a source of energy is undervalued in favor of polluting sources such as fossil fuels from sludge that has no intrinsic value, as it is primarily fermentation of biological wastes.

The artificial value given to gold, gems, and other metals serves more to reward investor greed than to reflect any intrinsic value, yet people have been known to steal and kill for it. Other than its applied value in manufactured products, these precious stones and metals would otherwise have no value beyond its appearances. A false premise of supply and demand exists which states that high demand creates high value. High demand does not create high value; greedy suppliers create high prices, while value remains unchanged.

For instance, if there were 1,000 pies, and one hundred persons, and the pies sold for one dollar each, then why should 10 pies sell for more than one dollar each? The value of the pies are constant; only the demand changes because of the perceived shortage, which when coupled with the greed factor increases the price of each pie. A pie is still a pie. What if few people liked pies? Then it could still be sold for one dollar, but few people would value it.

Civilization has now entered a new era of speculation. Stock prices have soared beyond the realm of reason, where the current P/E ratios of some stocks would take hundreds of years to return the initial stock price if based on actual performance. People gamble their life savings and retirement funds on stocks. Banks and insurance companies are required to have less than reserve, profit/loss ratios speculation, with high paper value, but risky real value. Eventually, food will become a political bargaining chip, and warfare for the sake of wealth building for the elites will encourage government collusion with wealthy powerbrokers. War has been repeatedly utilized by nations to take by force from other people what they could not procure by negotiation or bribery at the cheap price that they were willing to pay.

Middle-East oil interests make them worth going to war for protection of the flow of cheap oil to our factories, cities and refineries. Vietnam was disguised as an attempt to stop the spread of communism, while in fact the fear was that the communist hard line fanatics would refuse to negotiate the price of oil and raw materials found in S.E. Asia, and would further be an obstacle to the interests of the secret world government that is pushing the realization of the new world order. But now that the largest remaining communist nation is willing to deal on capitalistic terms, there is no longer a need or desire to go to war. The real issues are rarely simply ideological differences, but rather competing economic interest camouflaged by ideology.

PERSISTENT SOCIO-ECONOMIC PROBLEMS

The primary purpose of government is to preserve the status quo, to ensure that the wealthy are able to maintain or to increase their wealth at the expense of the general public, the mass of faceless statistical demographics of the consumer market.

From the moment an idea is conceptualized, the government implements complex laws, procedures, and expensive fees that give large corporations an unfair advantage over individuals who have new inventions. The stumbling blocks and obstacles permit corporations to literally steal or suppress potential patents that might be competitive with existing products.

While the government goes earnestly after criminals who violate copyrights by illegally duplicating movies, tapes, and CDs that are distributed by large corporations, little is ever done when these same corporations plagiarize songs, scripts, books, and music from individual artists. And if the struggling artists can't afford legal representation, then little if any action is ever pursued by the courts or by law enforcement.

When corporations invest resources to develop and market new products, they wish to be guaranteed a certain period of sales to allow a recapture of their investment capital and to make a sustained profit. Patent laws are structured to protect corporate interest because it deters individuals from easily introducing new products that make existing products obsolete. Oftentimes, it comes down to who has the best in-house law department who can persist in lengthy patents litigation. The effect of patent laws that provide little protection to individual inventors is to prevent the proliferation of new competitive products, thus maintaining the status-quo for an additional 2-5 years after inventors attempt to patent and market new products. Patents laws while purporting to protect the rights of all inventors are primarily written to permit large corporations to get the most profit out of a product, and are actually anti-invention and anti-innovation protection for the established market share of major corporations.

The legal obstacles to progress shows up in many forms, that keep society locked into a cycle of oil dependency, vehicle pollution, defense industry spending, and environmental pollution. Government pork barrel programs for the wealthy
abound as billions of dollars are spent on corporate farm subsidies, and other programs designed to discourage real competition. The long-standing strategy is to convince consumers to pay the same amount for fewer products, or to pay more for the same, and to call the difference supply and demand, or market rate.

The economic superpowers' role in improving world conditions is not selfless. The need to improve the economic condition of all people has the potential to develop new markets while improving the purchasing power of existing markets. Several basic problems require international cooperation to solve the historical problems of ethnic and racial warfare and continued overpopulation pressures on the ecosystem. The unequal distribution of the world's resources remain a source of global political uncertainties.

Technological solutions may turn out to be temporary placebos. The Y2K threat is the consequence of shortsighted application of a technological attempt to create greater efficiency and wealth. The continued trend to computerized global data may allow more accurate analysis of supply and demand forces to permit the appropriate distribution of resources to areas of greatest need.

The American federalist political system is in the need of a major overhaul. The replacement of old style politicians who owe special interest debts with those who are more representative of average constituencies will go a long way to defuse the increasing conflict that is the outcome of greater societal diversity and fragmentation. Phone/TV/internet interactive voting in real time during legislative sessions could result in more direct democratic participation. A real democracy could be possible from programs that cause the citizenry to become informed prior to voting by touch phone, computer or interactive television. The society is drowning from the weight of too many laws as all levels of government compound the legal codes with newer and more complex laws without eliminating old antiquated and inappropriate laws. As the society becomes more computerized, technocrats may eventually replace politicians in our governance.

The Globalization Paradigm - THE NEW WORLD ORDER (NWO)

The world is heading for a cashless financial basis. All the trade and financial transactions will eventually be done via the Internet, with fingerprint, retinal, computer chip, or bar code scanning (on forehead or hand) for identification. Already, the comprehensive computer files on the majority of Americans include credit history, criminal records, employment history, driving record, purchasing history via credit files or actual copies of checks, phone records, and computer coded postal records. These files are becoming merged into a master database. It would be a simple matter to key in each person's national I.D. number, such as a person's social security number, and to know every habit, time and date, of everyone who is part of the cashless societies of the near future. All of any person's known associates, friends, and family could be investigated within nanoseconds. Our politicians, government officials, and even law enforcement could be compromised, blackmailed, and dictated to by those with the access to and control of the worldwide personal database.

Once this financial computer network is finally in place, and all of the developed world's societies have acclimated to it, and have embraced it (as they are doing with the World Wide Web), then the true anti-Christ will show his head as the savior of the world. Once all trade and financial transactions become dependent on computers, the Internet, and electrical utility companies, the anti-Christ, a corporate technocrat who has blackmailed and bribed all of the world's major governments and leaders, will pull the plug on the Internet. This may come in the form of massive power outages at first, but later will be blamed on a computer virus (that they will create and can clean). World trade will come to a halt. The world's major economic powers will come to a standstill. People will riot in the streets as they starve. World leaders will beg the anti-Christ to relent, and he will emerge as the savior of mankind from its bleakest days, to form a singular world government to worship the Anti-Christ, who will stand up to do battle against the second coming of Christ, who will come back to earth from outer space, as part of an alien invasion.

The future of the world appears to be uncertain as famine, wars, disease, pestilence, social and political unrest will continue to persist globally. When President Bush, a senior member of the Trilateral Commission, continuously referred to "The New World Order", he was telling the world and its myriad of governments that the goal of the economic equity holders of the planet is to bring about a prosperous and profitable and relatively peaceful world (exceptions are when localized conflicts serve to boost the sale of military armaments, or the overthrow of unsympathetic governments is ordered by the secret world government).

In order to bring about an organized cooperative union of world governments for the primary benefit of the less than one percent of the people who own over sixty percent of the world's wealth and resources, certain social, political, and economic changes must be made to tear down the borders that have historically divided cultures, races, and religions.

The world's raw materials and resources must come under the sophisticated management of a world conglomerate who would oversee the inequitable distribution and allocation to the benefit of secret group of economic powerbrokers. After AIDS and other diseases (some natural, and a few manmade) devastates Africa (the crown jewel of the planet's natural resources), destabilizing its political and tribal loyalties, NWO members will "rebuild" Africa into various international barter zones where it's main commodities will be sold cheaply (or given away in various convoluted schemes that appear to benefit the poor and destitute, etc.) to NWO member corporations, governments, and individuals.

The world will become divided into various economic interest zones, to maximize its resources to provide raw materials, manufacturing labor, and product consumption. All of which will be coordinated to produce the maximum amount of profits to NWO member individuals and groups, whose identities will remain secret to deter violent retribution from "outlaw" groups, nations, and individuals who may desire to disrupt the new world order. For example, the following scenario may describe possible generalized economic zones of the NWO (this simplistic example is not meant to cast entire continents and its peoples into stereotypical generalities, but serves only as a scenario of a possible plan to redistribute and to exploit the world's resources and peoples to obtain optimal value and profitable return to the world's elitist equity holders that comprise less than one percent of humans).

Continent	Abundance of	NWO Role
Africa	natural resources	mining raw materials
Antarctica	icebergs/coldness	fresh water/research
Asia	people	cheap manufacturing
Australia	open land	grazing & growing
Europe	elites and assets	global rulers
No. America	military technology	global arms supplier
So. America	drug fields	corporate drug deals

The End times Scenario Paradigm

The world's 2 billion+ so-called Christians will be coerced and tricked into believing and following the anti-Christ as the true savior. Those who do not take the "666" computer chip will not be able to buy or sell anything because everything will be scanned by computers. The satellites will know where everyone who takes the "666" chip is at all times. The police will seek people who walk past public scanners who are not registered. Those who don't take the chip will be rounded up and imprisoned in the concentration camps that have already been built for the insurrections that will occur beginning in the year 2,000. After all the true Christians have been identified, they will be persecuted and/or killed for not taking the mark of the beast, the anti-Christ.

Satan is jealous of God and wants to prove that he Satan is as the God. In fact, he tempted Eve by telling her to eat from the forbidden tree of knowledge so she and Adam could be as smart as God. Since that time, mankind has been trying to be as smart as God. To be "all knowing", mankind has invented computers, cameras, vcrs, and satellites that can know anyone's location, credit history, driving record, medical history, employment history, purchasing habits, personal phone logs, and their most intimate thoughts.

To be like God, "who created man in His own image", mankind is now perfecting "cloning" techniques, and so he can replicate himself in "his own image." To be equal to God, mankind is trying to manipulate the DNA to find out how to make people live longer, and to discover ways to regenerate nerve tissue in the spinal column, then they could have "immortality" by cloning a person's body, then transplanting the head; thus, people who serve Satan can essentially live forever. To be "all powerful", mankind developed nuclear weapons to be able to destroy all life on earth. God wants man to be humble and to serve God, but man is taking the path to try to be equal to God, and consequently will serve Satan.

God will send his "angels" back to Earth, with "horseman and chariots" (space craft) descending from the heavens to attack and fight the armies from the Kings of the Earth, the One World Government, and the Anti-Christ. Asteroids and meteors will be dislodged from the Van Allen Asteroid belt beyond Mars and will be sent on crash paths to Earth to cause near extinction impacts. Earth will send its 6000 advanced pilotless joint attack fighter aircraft against the "alien extraterrestrial invaders" for the very survival of the human race. The ET's will release biological and chemical weapons of mass destruction and nuclear fires will destroy one-third of the world's vegetation, cities, animals, and people. Or perhaps, as terrorism gets out of control, nations and terrorist states escalate warfare into nuclear conflagration, chemical, biological, and genetic mass destruction.

No one can know the exact time of human extinction, but the seeds had already been planted from the times of the Great Christian Crusades against Islam. What we are seeing in the modern era is the natural evolution of hatred, jealousy, revenge, and intolerance between the world's governments and their culturally conditioned, manipulated and intolerant peoples. The major motivators of conflict and war are the struggles between the rich and the poor; the powerful and the powerless; zealous differences in religious dogmas between Christians, Jews, and Moslems; racial prejudice, ethno-centricity and cultural intolerance, and gender exploitation and subjugation. Remove the sources of conflict, and there could be cooperation and peace on Earth. Allow the sources of conflict to continue or become even more exacerbated, and there could be destruction and peace on Earth, without human beings.

Chapter 3 – Social Paradigm Shift

Lyndon LaRouche is likely correct about the impending financial collapse of the world system, but not simply due to bad economic policies driven by greed and political misjudgments and ignorant political and economic decision making by the state. Global economic collapse is the calculated outcome of deliberate world domination strategies of the secret reptilian world government to maintain the world's population as poor and powerless prey. The reptilians are far outnumbered by the apes. The reptilians are torn between their avarice destruction of world resources to feed their greed, and the demands of mass consumption by the developing nations.

The reptilian rulers want to reduce the numbers of apes to more manageable numbers, in order to preserve their power, and to protect the environment from the increasing pollution that is inevitable from an exploding world population, primarily of apes. By this strategy, the continued exploitation of limited world resources can serve to primarily benefit reptilians and their progeny. Conservation is not for the sake of saving apes, as apes are viewed as the major detrimental component of global environmental pollution.

What individuals and groups comprise the secret world government, we will likely never know (by lineages, specific names of living people), and particularly ideas on the battle between the forces of "good" and "evil", and how the lineages of "Cain" and "Able" have been entangled in the battle for earthly ascendancy. What do scientists really know about the reptilian genetic code that resides as part of *Homo sapien* DNA that is not found in apes? In other words, reptiles and apes are separate species, but natural disasters, like the near extinction asteroid strikes, scrambled stem cells from reptiles and apes that were in close proximity, and caused mutations among certain individuals, which began the "missing links" that eventually evolved into *Homo sapiens.* Consequently, certain sub-species of reptilian-homo sapiens came from the predatory reptiles, and others from non-predators. Apes also evolved into humans, however, their fetal development does not take them through the reptilian stage. This suggest that an intervening event likely occurred… perhaps the gene splicing of what became the missing link apes that became hominids and eventually humans.

The ape species is generally non-predatory, and very social, comprising the general masses of followers. The predatory reptilian-ape homo sapiens have ruled the world in a long lineage of kings, emperors, czars, rulers, and the world's elites because they are more "cold blooded" and aggressive. Apes are warm blooded and generally passive. You can observe these personality lineages differently in human beings. The Type "A" personality (not "A" for ape) is aggressive, cold hearted, angry, achieving ass-holes. They tend to be the leaders and CEOs of the world, comprised of the reptilian elites. On the other hand, the Type "B" personality (not "B" for butthead) is banal, brown-nosing, boring, and blind. They are the ape-like followers and true believers.

The reptilian types control the ape types, who serve the desires and decrees of the secret world governing reptilian order who own MNCs and rule nation-states, either as figure heads or as the power behind surrogates and puppets. Type AB are the non-predatory reptilian-ape hybrid human beings who are the non-aligned individualists, often the intellectuals or creative forces in societies. They are also the "captains" or surrogates of the ruling class. They are the managers and protectors of the infrastructure. They are the generals, creators, and caretakers of weapons of mass destruction. They are the bankers, economists, university professors, and aspiring politicians and entertainers who support the status quo system.

As an individual, what concerns me is three fold: (1) Can we, reptilians and apes, just get along? (2) If it's in the nature of the predatory lineage of reptiles to kill apes and other non-predatory reptiles, how big is their predatory appetite?, and (3) If apes and non-predatory reptiles join forces in numbers, can they really make a positive difference? To better understand the potential solutions to the future predatory slaughter of 4 billion human beings, we must address issues of the "soul". We must also ask if the "harvest of souls" might not in fact be a preordained plan of the extraterrestrials who initially seeded this planet Earth.

We must ask if the future return of the superior ETs for the Biblical "harvesting of souls" is actually the preordained method to join our human souls to God, or to collect our life force energies as a power source for their flying machines and for time travel. We earthlings are infants in the scheme of the universe, not even a blink of the eye in time. What is our true purpose? Why were we created? What is there after this physical life? What choices do we really have? There are many questions, and few answers that do not require an act of faith and belief in an unknown and uncertain schema... religion or cosmology.

We can fight, but there's no certainty of success. We can surrender, and there's no certainty of justice or mercy. We can die, and there's no certainty of resurrection or a better spiritual life. The economic system can collapse, and there's no certainty anything better will result. Or we can try to hang on to what we have, and there's no certainty things will get better, or that it won't collapse anyway. The only certain thing on this physical plane is pain and suffering for countless numbers of earthly inhabitants, both human and non-human that are born suffer, survive, and then die in the life/death cycle. We give and accept love. We become more or less aware of our environment, and sometimes empathize with the pains of injustice. Eventually, we die and become forgotten, as countless souls that blow in the wind, to be lost forever in the tides of time.

We live in a "matrix" that is much larger than any individual, group, or organization. The matrix is monitored, manipulated, and controlled by the secret world government. We are not powerless against the matrix, as we can write a sub-routine that creates a "bubble" to shield us from the negative effects and illusions of the matrix that allows us to operate somewhat clandestinely and independently of the matrix and its agents. But the matrix will still exist, until it's true creators return to change the matrix paradigm from what it is to what it is to become. I hope the change will be a good one. But nothing is certain, not even our deepest beliefs.

As a child, I used to go down to the railroad tracks (typical of many poor neighborhoods), to throw small rocks at the passing train box cars, watching them ineffectually bounce off with "banging" sounds. Some noise, but no affect... a few scratches, but not even a dent! That's how I generally view trying to "fight the system". I've witnessed civil protests from the fringes, and saw people beat up and arrested by the system's enforcers. Little ever changed. Maybe a few committees organized to occupy time, placate, confuse, and diffuse citizens' rage. That's all. Certainly, there have been eras when charismatic leadership inspired passionate mass cooperation and that led to violent revolutions in the past. And while the names changed, the game essentially remained the same.

As long as the world system is based upon "ownership" of land, raw materials, resources, labor, and technology, the best we can hope for is the replacement of oppressive regimes by less repressive regimes. It's a matter of degree, not substance. It's a matter of perspective, and not real structural change. Until there is genuine structural change, we will continue to read just another page in the same book. Is it possible to close the book? Is it possible to do something entirely different that changes the fundamental paradigm of our realities? It is possible. But it won't be easy. It would require a new alignment of world power relationships. It would require a new set of human motivations from materialism and greed to humanitarian and spiritual enlightenment. It would require that we arrest technology to permit the Earth to return to its natural balances.

We can keep computers and any devices that improve human communication and creativity without harming the natural environment. But human cloning, xeno-transplantation, interspecies hybrids, genetic and viral weapons development, and other unnatural inter and intra species experimentation must stop before we seed the mass annihilation of the entire human race, reptilians and apes alike. I ask, which would be more devastating, a collapse of the inequitable global economic system, the return of ETs to harvest human souls, or a manmade mass extinction of our human species to be replaced by new superior xeno-human hybrid species? I don't know.

The Right to Live, or the Right to Die Paradigm

The right to die and the right to live issues have been embroiled in legal and moral confusion, where in some states, the courts and law makers have become executioners, in others, saviors; and still others as protectors of free choice by women.

It is high time for the U.S. Congress to enact legislation that would provide uniform standards that make sense, providing adequate protection of privacy, freedom of choice, right to die and right to live across our gloriously free and democratic nation.

The issues are basic and simple, and should answer several fundamental questions:

1.   Do persons possessing legal capacity have the right to terminate their own lives at a time and in a manner of their own choosing; and is it legally permissible for physicians or other designated persons to assist in a humane suicide?

2. In cases where a person does not possess legal capacity to decide issues of life and death due to disabilities or incapacitation, does a legal or court-appointed guardian have the authority to terminate a human life, and if so, under what specific circumstances?

3. What entails artificial life support that could legally be terminated, when cessation of technological equipment would certainly lead to patient death?
   a. Heart-lung machine
   b. Kidney dialysis machine
   c. Pacemaker
   d. Feeding tube
   e. Trachea tube for breathing
   f. Appropriate medication, e.g. to prevent heart attacks

Certainly, in each case, denial of the assisted means of survival could be equivalent to a "de facto" death sentence, as surely as the denial of food and water would result in death.

4. Would denial of food and water to a disabled or terminally ill person be considered cruel and unusual punishment, if the same standard were to be applied to persons who would otherwise be in good health, e.g. "normal people"?

5. In the case of late term abortions, where the fetus would otherwise survive outside of the womb, does a woman have the right to abort and kill the fetus-infant? A proper C-section could, in most cases, save late term abortion fetuses, who could survive as most premature births do nowadays. If a life could survive on its own, then no one, not even the birthing mother has a right to terminate another human being.

The answer to these controversial questions should be based on a standard of sensibility and understanding of science, and strike a moral balance between the right to choose, and the sanctity of life that could survive without "extraordinary measures."

In the first instance, persons possessing legal capacity should have the right to commit suicide. To presume that life is worth living for every person, who after all was born without choice into circumstances not of their choosing, is presumptuous. Many people who suffer extreme physical and/or emotional pain would rather die than to prolong their pain. There are extraordinary circumstances where, despite medical, psycho-therapeutic, pharmacological, and technical assistance, a person may choose to commit suicide due to terminal illness, emotional or mental disorder, philosophical or spiritual commitment, or simply a profound dissatisfaction with life or their circumstances and environment.

In addition, the presence of medical professionals or laypersons to assist in the administration of humane methods of euthanasia, free of suffering, injury or trauma should be allowed. The alternative forms of suicide are the horrific, violent, and traumatic actions such as gunshot, stabbing, car crash, jumping off tall buildings, home electrocution, carbon monoxide poisoning by running car engine in closed garage, natural gas explosion in one's house, drug overdose, cutting wrists, and other bizarre methods only desperate people would do when severely despondent or in terrible pain.

In cases where incapacitation does not permit a person to insist or communicate their final wishes, and a legally enforceable living will does not exist, the court or legal guardian should be deemed the authority to terminate life, where extraordinary means must be employed. Extraordinary means would entail elaborate and expensive technological assistance that artificially prolongs life, such as heart-lung machines. All other technological low tech methods, equipment, or apparatus such as pacemaker, feeding tube, trachea breathing assistance, medication, or kidney dialysis should be considered "ordinary means" to "assist" life sustenance, which must not be withdrawn.

Consequently, the denial of food and water, which is basic to survival of all living beings, must be prohibited regardless of a person's disability, incapacitation or terminal illness, where the person or the legal guardian has made a choice to live. The denial of basic sustenance is a form of cruel and inhumane punishment (though it is not unusual in our world due to poverty and famine), and should be considered an immoral and illegal killing.

In cases of late term abortion, or where ordinary means would permit a fetus to survive on its own, termination of life should be illegal. This does not address the morality issues regarding a balance between a woman's freedom by choice versus the point of inception of a separate life. Scientific facts indicate that independent life begins when an entity is capable of its own survival, without attachment to a host entity, and without extraordinary medical or technological means.

If society, law makers, and the courts fail to apply a sensible uniform legal criteria to issues of abortion, euthanasia, assisted suicide, right to die, and right to live, then citizens will not enjoy the full protection of the U.S. Constitution, as life and death should not be a states rights issue, but instead our government should set a national and universal definition and standards. It is inherently unjust for life and death issues to be subjected to jurisdictional differences, where any citizens' chance of life or death depends upon location instead of uniform lawful principles.

NICE PEOPLE OR MEAN PEOPLE PARADIGM

We all go through life and are forced to deal with people one way or another, whether we want to, need to, like it or not. Generally, as we stumble through our life's path, we tend to meet primarily two types of people to various degrees on the continuum of behavior. A comparison of these two types of personalities shows a market contrast, with the hope that readers will recognize the connection between how certain people treat others and their *core character*.

NICE PEOPLE	MEAN PEOPLE
(often referred to as *suckers, wimps,* and *emotional weaklings*)	(*Alpha leaders*, users, tough emotionally/physically/mentally)

	NICE PEOPLE			MEAN PEOPLE
1.	Considerate		1.	Inconsiderate
2.	Compassionate		2.	Self-centered
3.	Humble		3.	Arrogant
4.	Selfless		4.	Selfish
5.	Cooperative		5.	Dictating
6.	Giving		6.	Demanding/taking
7.	Fearful/anxious		7.	Fearless/aggressive
8.	Innocent		8.	Predatory
9.	Insecure		9.	Over-confident
10.	Under-achiever		10.	Over-achiever
11.	Open-minded		11.	Opinionated
12.	Approval seeking		12.	Credit/recognition seeking
13.	Guilt complex		13.	Blameless/guiltless
14.	Self-deprecating		14.	Self-righteous
15.	Courteous		15.	Rude
16.	Moralistic/ethical		16.	Immoral/unethical
17.	Sacrificing		17.	Opportunistic
18.	Apologetic		18.	Ass kicking
19.	Helpful disposition		19.	Obsessed with winning
20.	Kind		20.	Manipulative
21.	Honest		21.	Deceptive
22.	Mellow/easy-going		22.	Angry and driven
23.	Patient		23.	Impatient
24.	Loyal		24.	Situational
25.	Supporting		25.	Leading

26.	Status quo maintainer	26.	Creator or destroyer
27.	Goes with the flow	27.	Their way or the highway
28.	Feels used/unappreciated	28.	Feels never enough due
29.	Worries about others	29.	Worries about self
30.	A friend you can trust	30.	Just another asshole

Additional Differences Between Nice versus Mean People

Observation: Mean people seek out nice people because they tend to be users, abusers, and predators. They possess a more pronounced *hunter instinct* that's hereditarily akin to animals. These *"alphas"* define, drive, and destroy our world, which otherwise would *"be too nice."* Nice people desire peace, freedom, brotherhood, family, love, civility, human dignity, human rights, and prefer to obey the law. Mean people want power, control, money, exploitation of others, self-centeredness, materialism, and don't like following society's rules, as they desire to be above the law. Following are some secondary distinctions between nice and mean people:

NICE PEOPLE		MEAN PEOPLE	
1.	ethical conduct	1.	amoral or immoral
2.	peaceful resolution seeking	2.	violence prone
3.	loyal	3.	disloyal
4.	open-minded	4.	rigid and opinionated
5.	willing to admit mistakes	5.	self-righteous
6.	tolerant and accepting of others	6.	intolerant and prejudice
7.	sincere	7.	manipulating
8.	trusting	8.	distrusting
9.	dependable	9.	unreliable
10.	predictable	10.	unpredictable
11.	honest and trustworthy	11.	deceptive

12.	creator, supporter, maintainer	12.	destroyer
13.	forgiving	13.	revengeful
14.	loving and kind	14.	angry, hateful and stingy
15.	accepting of differences	15.	racist and prejudice
16.	sexually considerate	16.	promiscuous, aggressive
17.	facts and situations change	17.	only relevant facts count
18.	intelligence is developed	18.	intelligence is inherited
19.	freedom is avoiding control	19.	control is power
20.	good health is prevention	20.	superior health is genetic
21.	money is functional	21.	money is control power
22.	accepts aging process	22.	wants to live forever
23.	being average is acceptable	23.	wants to be elitist
24.	wealth is desirable but unlikely	24.	wealth is desirable
25.	religious tolerance	25.	organized religion
26.	beauty's only skin deep	26.	beauty can be purchased
27.	say what is appropriate	27.	"say what I wanna say"
28.	do what is appropriate	28.	"do what I wanna do"
29.	eat enough to satisfy hunger	29.	"eat what I want"
30.	sex is love and intimacy	30.	"screw whoever I want"
31.	go where affordable	31.	"go where I want"
32.	rules restrain animal urges	32.	"rules don't apply to me"
33.	avoid trouble by knowing limits	33.	test system, push limits
34.	persuade others to cooperate	34.	outsmart and command
35.	be humble in achievement	35.	win at all cost, then brag
36.	conserve for a rainy day	36.	get other people's share
37.	living is a gamble everyday	37.	gamble on high risk
38.	be fair and reasonable	38.	aggressive and attack
39.	others welfare is important	39.	no body else matters
40.	plan for the future	41.	react forcefully

There are many other significant difference between people who prefer to be nice and considerate versus those who often get their way by being mean, demanding, and selfish. Here's a description of a person, whom you may recognize among your associates or family members. This person may appear to be fictional, but it's a mild illustration of the heightened tension and drama that personifies many typical "mean-spirited" people. Oftentimes, nice people may feel the following describes people who are "crazy" or "bi-polar", but whatever euphemism is used, the actions are similar and fall into the pattern of meanness.

1. Make decisions impulsively and impatient for gratification
2. Insist on self correctness and doggedly defends position, stubborn
3. Changes mind on direction of action depending upon mood and impulse
4. Insults people if their views are in opposition, calling them stupid
5. Repetitious of certain favorite stories or phrases from their life experience
6. Self-indulgence in "everything", and highly self-centered
7. Sometimes rewards a select few who complement and tolerates idiosyncrasies
8. Blames others if things don't work out her way
9. Takes contrary view, or criticizes other's positions, just to find faults
10. Expects people to say and do things "her way"
11. Intolerant of interruptions, as what she says is always important to herself
12. Challenges other people's "facts" as conjecture and suppositions
13. Historical view with little futuristic orientation or broad view of the world

14. High risk behaviors and risk seeker
15. Fearless when having the upper hand
16. Revengeful and aggressive
17. Obsessive and compulsive
18. Triggers to high verbal volatility and aggressive profane barrages
19. Disinterested in other's views, which are considered unimportant or stupid
20. Competition, if personally affected wants to win at all cost
21. Racist view of world, interpersonal relations, and social economic order
22. Punitive; threat oriented when feeling in charge, control freak
23. Resist expressing "positive" emotions as sign of weakness
24. Contradictory morality or immoral
25. Rebellious against others who attempt to exercise influence or control
26. Leaves her fate blowing in the wind and will try anything if in the mood
27. Doesn't give a damn, even if the worse consequences are possible
28. Not compassionate, it's other people's own fault for bad things happening
29. Manipulative, and will befriend if potential benefits in various ways
30. Disloyal to family and loved ones, and unfaithful to lover; opportunistic
31. Secretive, tells you what she wants you to know or think, not often the truth
32. Highly calculating and manipulative of immediate environment
33. Highly exploitive in diverse and changing situations

34. Realistic and pragmatic view and approach to using people for self gain
35. Inability to feel guilt, and or to love deeply
36. Attracted to superficial appearances, like candy in a store
37. Able to withstand high degree of physical pain and punishment
38. Feels she deserves to be a served and kiss-up to by others
39. Desires total freedom and no commitment, "have casual sex with who she wants, eat what she wants to eat, go when she wants to go, and do what she wants to do, etc."
40. Persistent, compulsive, obsessive, extreme, and determined at all cost

Ironically, both nice people, as well as mean people are attracted to nice people. Nice people enjoy being around nice people because it's a time for sharing, caring, communications, relaxation and enjoyment. Mean people want to be around nice people in order to be served, to take advantage, boss others around, get nice people to do things they are either too lazy to do, or don't feel like doing. And when mean people don't get their way immediately, they tend to yell, insult, and express rage like spoiled brats who never grew up emotionally. Unfortunately, those who rise to the top of organizations tend to be these mean-spirited and driven ass-holes because they refuse the alternative of going along with others, instead of always getting their own way.

These mean-spirited predators feel no shame or guilt in backstabbing competitors, associates, friends, or family if anyone gets in their way of achieving their compulsive goals. Often, they get so used to others giving in to their demanding manner, that they don't even think they're being inconsiderate or mean. It never crosses their mind that they are the source of conflict and discomfort to others, because most people are willing to let mean people have their way, just to avoid all the unnecessary drama and conflict, usually over stupid and unimportant issues. And even when aggressive people realize they are being jerks, they enjoy the feeling of having power and control over others, making others run around like trained dogs. The feeling of power and invincibility is an aphrodisiac that reinforces mean people's rude behavior, and therefore it would be very foolish of nice people to ever expect mean people to change their stripes because they gain too much benefit from their instinctive predatory behavior.

If all the nice people could someday band together and force mean people to change their ways, to be more humane and less despicable, the societies in the world would be a much nicer place, where people could become more fulfilled and happy. Unfortunately, it's the mean people who rule the world, own the world's resources, command governments and militaries, and enforce laws that keep them in control of the world's nice and meek people. The historical world paradigm has not been one of "survival of the fittest," but instead, "survival of the meanest." And perhaps that paradigm will never change in our lifetime because nice people will always give in to mean people, if for no other reason than to avoid conflict, and have some peace.

Mean people will rarely if ever change. It's too convenient and simple to be predatory and mean as a practical tactic to reap benefits from nice people who are viewed as being weak. IT WORKS!!! When mean people are forced to deal with other mean people, they often attack each other like pit bull dogs, and both come out of the fight bruised and bloodied because each wants to be the dominant dog. Whether winner, loser, or tied, mean people will seek out nice people to help them to heal their wounds... and they demand service or they'll throw fits. Nice people beware! Being around mean people is bad for nice people's health, wealth, and happiness. Get lost quick!

THOUGHTS FOR THE DAY

- The wise person is the one who knows when to avoid the wise guys. Setting reasonable and attainable goals leads to success and fulfillment. The grass is not always greener on the other side, especially if it's smoked.
- Children need role models to help formulate behavior, but adults just need to behave.
- If you want something real bad, it's probably an addiction and not just a passion
- Help thy neighbor and you are not likely to be forgotten, as they are likely to ask again and again.
- Look not for validation from others, as even fools will applaud you from time to time.
- If you are asked, "what's your name" it's only because people want to get personal.
- High-strung people have a difficult time getting their guitars tuned.
- When in doubt, listen for the right answer. When you think you're absolutely right, listen a lot more.
- The customer is not always right, but you can be always wrong in their eyes.
- The best way to avoid conflict is not to take things way too seriously.
- Character is not about being able to stand up to stronger forces, but being strong enough to stand up after being knocked over.
- It's easy to get angry at others for small inconveniences or insults but difficult to have the calmness to overcome large challenges and threats.
- If our daily affairs were so easy to achieve, then we should let chimps do our jobs.

- Cats have nine lives, rabbits are lucky and dogs bark louder than their bites. What do people have going for them?
- When the chickens first come home to roost, there tends to be a lot of squawking and activity but few eggs are ever laid.
- Organization is putting things in mental and physical boxes so you can find them in the dark with your eyes closed.
- Efficiency is trying to get the most for the least… similar to capitalism.
- If you have a bubble to burst, you can bet that someone will surely do it for you.
- Look not to others for judgment for surely they shall judge you in accordance to the benefits that they do not get from you.
- Charity starts at home because it's a great training ground to prove oneself.
- Anyone who feels superior to others suffers from self-doubt and self-image insecurity. Otherwise, why would they even bother to compare?
- CARE = Concern After Realizing Errors.
- The bull runs downhill but the buck stops here.
- We rarely live completely the lives we want, but typically live the lives we need.
- Charities begins at home, but in an abusive environment, leave quickly.
- Sincerity is never having to convince anyone that you really are.
- It's easier to be honest, unless you have an extraordinarily accurate memory.
- If people tell you they love you, ask them to prove it.
- When you feel down, drink 2 beers and sing your favorite song on You Tube.
- Depression happens when the feeling of failure becomes overwhelming.

- Why worry about how you appear to others if they don't write your paycheck?
- Violent people act out for various reasons... just don't give them any excuses.
- If you expect fairness and equality, try going to paradise or heaven.
- It's nobody's job to make you happy.
- Happiness is simply a decision not to be unhappy.
- Givers are not takers and takers are not givers.
- When in doubt, do nothing until you gather sufficient information to decide.
- The stress and pressures of day-to-day life is nothing compared to catastrophe.
- Mind over matter... if it doesn't matter, you wouldn't mind.
- Love is an expression given, but to have an impact, it must first be appreciated.
- People want what they don't have instead of being happy with what they have.
- Young people want to be older, and old people want youth.
- It's okay to be anonymous, unnoticed, unperturbed and at peace with oneself.
- Being unknown is being un-owned.
- If you ardently believe in anything, you set yourself up for unexpected surprises.
- People cheer you when they think you're one of them, even if you're really not.
- Illusions are what society is all about because truth hurts too much.
- How do we change the world for the better? Start with yourself.

Chapter 4 – Economic Paradigm Shift

How Most of the Super Rich Made It: EXPOSED!

We've all heard the stories of rags to riches, networking, hard work, luck, education, talent, determination, and skills as paths to success and wealth. Let's face it folks. Just look around you, and I bet you regularly see lots of people who are working hard, networking, well-educated, talented, determined, and have ample skills in many fields. So why aren't they rich? Let's forget the basic fact that one-third of people simply were born with a platinum spoon in their mouths. Then, let's forget about the other one-third who got lucky with their investment portfolios and sold out before the markets crash. That leaves the one-third who own businesses, and have built bank accounts, organizations, and corporations, often from scratch. How do *some* of these "smart" and successful entrepreneurs do it? (We're sure the vast majority of business owners, CEO's, and investors are almost totally ethical and honest, and wouldn't think to take advantage of any competitors, customers, or innocent fools).

The Wealth Paradigm

You probably learned that business success is all about hard work, honesty, persistence, determination, talent, market savvy, good timing, good products, competitive pricing, good dependable and honest helpers (workers), and the developing a good reputation. That's probably the "right" way to succeed.

The simple reality is the "fast track" to success for those who are impatient or too greedy to do it the hard way. The secret way to success is a path that is filled with trickery, where innocents are convinced, tricked, deceived, and otherwise persuaded to sign their names on pieces of paper called contracts, agreements, deeds, or whatever will transfer their small fortunes into the control and portfolio of the slick and greedy middlemen who act as brokers.

Take for example the exorbitant commissions that are made by dealmakers and brokers for the mega-mergers, easily amounting to billions of dollars, just for getting two parties to sign some papers. By the way, notice that several major rounds of employee lay-offs follow all mega mergers? Let's not even look at the mega deals. If you can get enough people to sign away their small assets on a routine basis, eventually, you'll end up with a pot of gold at the end of the rainbow.

There's Method to the Madness. Things are rarely what they seem, and seem rarely what they really are. It is much easier to get ill from believing too much, than from a healthy dose of realistic cynicism. The following strategies are not in any order, and application depends on the business situation. We don't recommend the use of these tactics; however, we think you should be aware of them, as they're being used by the unscrupulous on a daily, hourly, and minute-by-minute basis.

Quick and Unscrupulous Strategy to Wealth

- When planning to do something wrong, evil, illegal, greedy, predatory, or dishonest, first create a diversion; a fire, conflict, or non-issue to focus others attention away from your surreptitious and secretive activities. If you should get caught (the chances of getting caught for sophisticated "white-collar" crime is less than 1% than getting caught for a speeding ticket), deny it, then try to place the blame on others whom you've set up in advance to be the "patsies", fall guys, or scapegoats.

- Spy on your competitors. Better yet, spy on your allies, as their guards will be down. Obtain compromising information, photos, videos, tape recordings and other secrets, then use the information to your advantage (it's become very easy to spy with today's technology and professional spying companies).

- Extort your so-called friends, allies, and competitors by threatening to expose their secrets or scandalous activities. Leak a small sample to the press to show that you're capable of acting on your threats if they don't cooperate. Keep pressure on competitors and foes by constantly attacking them to keep them busy and on the defensive, while your agents and spies infiltrate from the rear guard. Ideally, use proxies who cannot be overtly tied to your efforts.

- Bribe vulnerable people to make them into traitors within the camps of both friends and foes, causing them to compromise their positions. Make detailed records for future leverage and extortion. Use the media and schools to convince the population of one's innocence and victimization to garnish sympathy, which is used to weaken public resistance and to engender patronage and charity.

- Get your agents, proxies, and insiders appointed or hired into key positions in arenas of wealth and power, top executive, political, and government positions and key "hub" or "gate keeping" corporate and bureaucratic positions to maximize intelligence gathering and manipulation. The pivotal positions for control and espionage would be: Chairman of the Board, Director on the Board President, VP, CEO, COO, CFO, Executive Secretary/Assistant, Personal Assistant/Advisor, Department Head, Under-Secretary of various government departments and agencies, Ambassador, CIS/MIS Director, and any department that handles sensitive and secretive information.

- If you can get your people up to the very top, the Senate, Governorship, Vice President, or President of our government, YOU SCORE A BIG COUP! Notice none of these positions are rank and file, middle or low-level jobs. It's ONLY at the very top of organizations where the greatest amount of CONTROL, damage, embezzlement, misappropriation, spying, and deception can be done.

- Control communications and networking technology and records. Have many "back doors" to allow spying and recording of scandalous conversations and secrets that would compromise targeted parties. Obtain the "inside track" and use insider information to maximize advantage in financial transactions, investments, mergers, government contracts, drug trafficking, money laundering, and other ill-gotten activities through key personnel and confederates at all relevant positions at all levels. Never snitch on your own people, and always work to keep them out of jail or from exposing your plans, methods, and secrets.

- Assassinate (or cause "accidents") to double-crossers, as an example to instill fear in one's organization, and for revenge. Destroy innocent people if necessary or convenient to blame your enemies, and to foster public enmity upon your competitors and foes. Spread vicious rumors, lies, misinformation, and propaganda disguised as facts and news against those who get in the way of your agenda.

- Keep secret back door relations with members of the enemies of your larger foes and competitors, but maintain "deniable distance". Act to benefit only those in one's group by elevating them to the highest positions possible, or if not possible, appear to support outsiders in exchange for reciprocal future returns.

- Try to blend in with the majority, by changing ones appearance and surnames to minimize prejudice, to increase opportunity, and decrease discovery.

- Obtain the support of so-called "experts" to ridicule, discredit and ostracize your foes and competitors, to shed a negative light on them with the public.
- Confuse the public as to what is real and what is fiction, to keep them from recognizing and reacting correctly against your true secret agendas.
- Brainwash the children of your allies and foes to cause disunity, conflict, and destructive competition. Your goals is to have them wipe each other out, or be too busy to recognize you moving in for the kill and take over.
- Change the rules when they don't provide sufficient benefits. Get your hired guns, lawyers, and lobbyists to make new rules and laws, which punish your foes and competitors, while increasing your share of the pie.
- Publicize the few occasions of apparent public charity to cover up one's true avarice and advancement. Appearing to be benevolent is great, especially if there are tax loopholes and deductions of benefit. Good PR for the future.
- Do the opposite of what you say, and say the opposite of what you'll do, but be sure to put a positive spin on it. Make sure the public perception is that you're a victim of circumstances, and had to be flexible for justifiable and rational reasons. Don't get caught looking like a liar and promise breaker! The public has a relatively short memory anyway, not usually greater than one month time.
- Help others only when it would bring you a ten-fold return, opening new opportunities to benefit your agenda in the future.
- Rename everything and make everything so complex that outsiders can't figure out what you're really doing. Skim or embezzle as much as possible, and transfer the funds into offshore havens. Get some clever accounting and tax attorneys to figure out how to avoid paying taxes with various tax shelters and tax avoidance scams.

- Get away with as much possible before you're eventually discovered. Hide as much as possible through secret offshore numbered accounts, real estate, and other transactions using business fronts and proxies. If you finally get caught, escape to a country of asylum that hates America (but that means you'll likely have to bribe corrupt government officials and politicians in some despotic Third World county... which is not much different from what you would otherwise be doing at home anyway).

- Use people to the max for cheap, or for free if possible. Then move on to greener pasture when people discover they're being used, and revolt. If you repeat the same deceptions often enough, simply changing cities, addresses, names, company logos, and product line or services should keep you very well insulated from ever getting caught.

- This is by no means an exhaustive list of wealth building strategies that are operative in the real world. With the sophistication of technology and the pervasiveness of computers, even bored housewives (do we still have those in America?) can now learn to supplement their incomes with a few "tricks" (without leaving one's bedroom).

- As long as we live in a culture that glorifies wealth, forgives greed, and admires people who are "smart enough" to fool the "system", then ample opportunities prevail for cheaters, because the blood of the innocents has already paved the path to riches.

- Then again, you can always do it the way we think success should be done. Success in business should be based upon hard work, honesty, persistence, determination, talent, market savvy, good timing, good products, competitive pricing, good dependable and honest helpers (workers), and the developing a good reputation. That's probably the "right" way to succeed.

- But then, try telling that to those whose business practices are on the "fast track to riches." They'd think you are foolish and naïve, and perhaps very stupid. There's not a chance that people would give up on making "easy money" just to feel they could claim to be honest and forth right, and unsuccessfully broke. Go figure. This is how things work in the real world. The structure of the world rewards deception. Any murderer would be out of their mind to plead guilty and place their fate at the mercy of the court.

Future Economic Perils in the American Economy

Our domestic economy is comprised of 80+ percent by service sector jobs, which indicates it is primarily based on people relying on others to do what they lack the adequate skills, time, or desire to achieve. It's an economy based upon an abundance of ignorance, laziness, and conveniences. Common sense would suggest that ignorance, laziness and convenience are not precursors of a competitive economic system in a global paradigm, as compared to economics based upon knowledge expertise, effort, and perseverance.

The infrastructure and relationships within the American economy may portend an inherent weakness toward eventual and sudden collapse, as artificial stock, employment, and monetary value bubbles burst. Critics would argue that the American economy is the strongest that the modern world has ever seen, with GDP approaching $15 trillion annually. However, several recent events indicate the U.S. economy is subject to severe fluctuations, such as those which almost bankrupted several economic sectors after the "911" terrorist attacks, in addition to the "dot-com" collapse only a year earlier.

Let's examine a plausible scenario based upon current economic and geo-political trends. Germany, France, and all European nations share a common monetary system. Great Britain (UK), pressured by economic necessity, would eventually join the E.U. China's burgeoning growth, coupled with Japan's capitalization has the potential to become a regional partnership powerhouse in Asia, each holding vast sums of American dollars, together producing the majority of products consumed by Americans.

Americans may dread the day when a united EU-UK, coupled with a united Asia, with Russia as a bi-lateral trading partner of both, cooperate to provide economic pressure against the United States. Juxtaposed against this dire economic backdrop could be unrelenting conflict in the Middle East, as Arabs continue to resist Israeli power and the international Jewish agenda of domination of global economic resources. The consequences of heightened Jewish economic power and Israeli military power could bring about another oil crisis, as Arab states retaliate against supporters of the Jewish state. Already, the U.S. relies almost entirely on foreign manufacturers to produce a dozen strategic components required by its most advanced military systems. Americans are becoming increasingly dependent on less expensive imports to offset a drop in real purchasing power, as U.S. corporations continue to build factories and export American jobs overseas or south of the border to cheap labor markets.

The internal economy upon which U.S. GDP (gross domestic product) data accrues is comprised by measuring the spending of American consumers, investors, government, and net exports. Carving up the mythical $15 trillion annual U.S. GDP indicates that government spending (federal, state, local, etc.) accounts for over $5 trillion, consumerism for another $5 trillion, and investments of about $5 trillion annually. A projected federal deficit of $450+ billion (not to mention states), and a deepening trade deficit exceeding $450 billion suggest that our domestic economic bubble is comprised to a great extent on illusory spending.

It is estimated that foreign interests, individuals, groups and nations, such as Saudi Arabia, China, and Japan, own about $2 trillion in U.S. currency and bonds. In addition, many foreign and multi-national corporations (MNCs) directly own or control in excess of $2 trillion invested in American corporations and real estate portfolios. What might happen to the U.S. economy were certain foreign interests to make sudden enormous liquidation of U.S. currency, stocks, bonds, and real estate investments? A rapid spiraling drop in consumer confidence would surely follow such wholesale destructive market movements. In 1997, the manipulation of billions of dollars of hedge funds by a single man, George Soros, greatly contributed to the near collapse of the Asian monetary exchange market, contributing to severe devaluation of the value of domestic currencies in Indonesia, Malaysia, Korea, and other SE Asian countries. Could a similar scenario happen right here in the United States of America? A large coordinated attack against the U.S. dollar could cripple the American economy, and drive the U.S. into a severe economic depression, with only the treat of worldwide thermonuclear war as a subsequent and real deterrent against foreign economic domination or invasion.

The fundamental question remains; "Does the U.S. have the capacity to survive independently of international trade, were our current trading partners to become our trading competitors or enemies instead?" What could happen if foreign governments such as Saudi Arabia and other oil producing nations were to conspire to "de-dollarize" their oil exports, such that U.S. dollars would no longer be accepted as payment for crude oil? Would the U.S. be forced to drain our precious oil reserves, then trade our limited gold and transfer military hardware and technology in barter for oil? Certainly, under such circumstances, the U.S. economy would immediately go into shock, with run-away inflation that will create an out-of-control cycle of massive job loss, plummeting stock market values, widespread personal and business bankruptcies, and destruction of capital and capital assets.

Under such a scenario, the U.S. economy would experience a paralysis not seen since the Great Depression of the 1930's, and would call for Uncle Sam to start another round of FDR-style public employment programs to save the economy. But where would the federal government find tax dollars to spend? States and local governments would become bankrupt, and there would be insufficient taxes collected from the shrinking employed population to fund any ambitious government-backed employment program. A precursor of America's future economic problems may be experienced by California (arguably the sixth largest economy in the world), as its bonds are now valued just above "junk" by bond rating companies. Is it conceivable that U.S. government bonds could also become "junk" someday? Simply printing more money to pay off existing bonds and debts held by foreign investors would not clear the ledger, without causing the complete collapse and rejection of the dollar abroad.

Were such a global conspiracy among our potential competitors and foes to materialize, what could the U.S. government do to survive, while leading Americans back into solvency? Already, multi-national corporations approach the world as one global marketplace, without any loyalty to nation, creed, or politics. Profit making and profit taking is all that drives the global economy, as capitalism without any morals or consideration of future perils. America's largest corporations have taken on the appearance of moneymaking vehicles to return exorbitant CEO compensation packages, to the detriment of both stockholders and employees.

Corporate profits are often not reinvested back into the domestic economy in the form of stockholder dividends, new hiring, and investment in buildings and equipment. Instead, profits are taken out of the U.S., and hidden in offshore tax-free havens, or invested overseas in nations with low standards of living with abundant cheap labor. How does irresponsible corporate actions contribute to strengthening the American economy? It doesn't, and instead, places America in potential economic peril.

How can our government protect us against such worse case scenarios? The recent federal efforts to stimulate the economy has had limited and sporadic success. Lowering the federal discount rate certainly has benefited banks and financial institutions, has encouraged home purchasing (but inflated home prices more than offsets lower mortgage interest rates) and loan refinancing, and has somewhat stimulated car purchasing, but it has not resulted in more jobs that would provide more spendable income for average Americans. The lower cost of borrowing money is not producing real gains because corporations and wealthy individuals are not reinvesting the surplus capital into the domestic economy, and continue to lay off thousands of workers as part of corporate strategy to enhance CEOs' stock options. The tax cut, while well intentioned to provide more discretionary dollars to consumers is easily absorbed by runaway credit card debts and increased housing costs. The added $300-$600 tax break for most wage earners doesn't cover the added cost of consumer debt, as the tax cut is primarily a transference of money from wage earners to creditors, lenders, and landlords. The most important issue apparently being missed by Greenspan, the currency czar, is the continued loss of consumer confidence that results from a fear of job loss. As more workers lose confidence in the longevity of their jobs, they tend to abstain from making large purchases, and try to hang on to the little savings that they have for that stormy period that seems to linger on the horizon.

It's becoming urgent for the U.S. to develop economic targets that can be realistically achievable by the U.S. economy, against the larger backdrop of global competition. What economic policies could effectively turn around a sluggish economy while protecting its foundation against future peril and attacks? Firstly, we must develop a national vision of our economic future, set goals, and put into place national strategies to grow the economy while protecting against inflation, deflation, high unemployment, wild stock market speculation, higher budget deficit spending, and the transference of wealth to international conglomerates and speculators who have not qualms about robbing the life out of America for short-term gains.

We must not rely solely on tax cuts and lower interest rates to stimulate the economy because middle class consumers benefit relatively slightly, while the wealthy and corporate elites have not shown a desire to reinvest excess profits back into their commercial enterprises in America. Without placing substantial discretionary funds into the pockets of wage earners, coupled with increasing belief that the public will have jobs, consumers will hesitate to spend. Without added spending, economic activity remains sluggish and any systemic shock or external attacks against the economy would likely cause a slide into a significant recession, and possible economic depression.

America must become more independent of foreign trade to obtain manufactured goods. The U.S. must gain direct benefits from their occupation of Iraqi oilfields to stabilize oil prices. Agricultural products should be supported as a major source to balance our trade deficit, and to act as an anchor to ensure that our trading partners will continue to accept the U.S. dollar as payment for their imported goods. High tech industries, defense programs, biotechnologies, pharmaceuticals, and scientific research must be supported and freed from excessive red tape. These fields provide the foundation for future economic growth, protection against foreign competitors, and a safety margin against terrorism and conspiracies against the American economy, while improving the quality of life for current and future generations of Americans.

Immigration must be controlled, and all illegal foreign nationals must be identified, rounded up, and deported, which will decrease the demand for expensive infrastructure services by almost 10 million people. Saving vast amounts wasted on public spending for education, healthcare, social services, law enforcement, and incarceration of illegal immigrants would result in restoring local and state governments to solvency.

The public education system must be revamped and redesigned to provide the highly educated and trained professional that is required by high tech, defense and scientific industries. We can no longer accept a broken public school system that produces the lowest performers among western nations. As long as our public school system continues to turn out students who are basically ignorant, lazy, and seekers of conveniences, we will continue to be trapped in an economy that depends on the purchase of services to compensate for mass stupidity.

It is essential for mass media to take a more responsible path that contributes to improving society, rather than to encourage and exploit scandals, human conflict, and baser escapists drives for the sake of advertising dollars and commercial profits. Television, movies, and computer games have become the media of destruction, where fun is equated to massive destruction, killing, profanity, and disregard for moral and responsible conduct. Our youth are being programmed into destroyers, who are able to delve inordinate hours in fantasy instead of spending time creating worthwhile things, pursuing constructive activities, or supporting their communities. This continuing trend is not healthy for a civilization that is becoming ever less civilized, and without a civil and educated citizenry, who will be capable of maintaining a complex high tech economy of the future, we may be doomed to suffer the consequences of our present failures.

We need to minimize the adversarial relationships within our government. Much political conflict results from factions who spend inordinate time, energy, and expense to sabotage their competitors' legislative and political agendas. The drive for power, and to win at all cost invariable leads to a destructive course where personality innuendoes, and not public issues become the fodder of the day. The supposed healthy public discourse rarely materializes, and instead is replaced by tidbits of media sound bites designed for the comprehension and consumption of fourth graders. Democracy becomes muffled by rumors, misstatements, and media biases. There's a time for competition (hopefully without dirty tricks, slander, and scandals), but more often, there's more reason to invest time on finding cooperative common grounds for solving the people's problems.

The people want answers and solutions, much more than the political squabbling and infighting that seems to typify our government leaders. Give the people what they want, a stable and prosperous economy based upon a capitalist market system that is not corrupted by excessive greed, fraud and dishonesty. Our genius federal forefathers designed a political and economic system of the people, for the people, and by the people. Let's ensure that proper actions are taken to safeguard this great nation, America, against the economic perils of the present and future.

Preventing Economic Perils in the American Economy

Our domestic economy is based upon service sector employment, which accounts for more than 80% of all American jobs, which indicates people rely heavily on others to do what they lack the adequate skills, time, or desire to achieve. It's an economy based upon an abundance of ignorance, laziness, and conveniences. Common sense would suggest that ignorance; laziness and convenience are not precursors of a competitive economic system in a global paradigm, as compared to economics based upon knowledge expertise, effort, and perseverance.

The infrastructure and relationships within the American economy may portend an inherent weakness toward eventual and sudden collapse, as artificial stock, employment, and monetary value bubbles burst. Critics would argue that the American economy is the strongest that the modern world has ever seen, with GDP approaching $15 trillion annually, offset by its National Debt reaching $15 trillion. However, several recent events indicate the U.S. economy is subject to severe fluctuations, such as those which almost bankrupted several economic sectors after the "911" terrorist attacks, in addition to the "dot-com" collapse only a year earlier.

As the world entered a new millennium, we began a new era filled with uncertainty. Old problems that weren't solved during the twentieth century returned to shatter our lives during the first few years of the twenty-first century. The Y2K meltdown never materialized, partly due to the hundreds of millions of dollars expended to rewrite trillions of lines of computer codes, and also due to relatively easy fixes provided to the Microsoft PC platforms. Then came the "dotcom" crashes, followed by the horrific confidence collapsing terrorist attacks of "911", a year of artificially induced energy shortages that inflated prices, corporate corruption scandals, and the war in Iraq. Our economy began the new millennium on a rollercoaster ride with unforeseen curves, ups and downs, along with hair raising and heartbreaking drops for average wage earners, pension funds, and stock market speculators and investors. Consumers, employees, stockholders, and employers all lost confidence as deception and speculation, instead of facts and sensibility ruled the marketplace.

The potential paralyzing effects of catastrophic events such as the "911" terrorist attacks served both as an economic "wake-up call" against America's false sense of security and self-reliance, and a reminder that unforeseen and uncertain circumstances will likely manifest negative anticipatory economic outcomes. Despite America's initial rapid military success in the Iraq campaign, growing insurgency, lingering instability and uncertainty has tainted our military victory. The economic development plans for Iraq and the potential gains for America remain unclear; a consequence of not having comprehensive post-war plans in place before the war.

On the home front, workers continue to fear future lay-offs as corporate America has shed over 3 American million jobs since the dawning of the new millennium. Corporate CEO's justify their belt-tightening measures as technology, executive greed, international competition, off shore contracts, and wild stock market fluctuations have eliminated those American jobs forever. The revelations about corporate corruption along with business bankruptcies have sent a chill down the spines of investors and wage earners alike.

Everyone desperately seeks an economic crystal ball, at least to have reliable trend data and forecasting to permit them to better assess their current and future investment and employment options and choices. Investors look for sure ways to protect their assets, as the average workers are growing concerned about protecting their asses. People in every sector of the economy are looking for answers, a few bright spots, and any apparent "sure thing" that might come along. What experts and commoners have all neglected to recognize is the continuing force of old habits on a world that has moved onward to another place in time. Coping with the current realities and predicting the next trends are essential realities that everyone must consider to increase their opportunities for success, and to avoid the potentially catastrophic losses from great failures. What can we derive from economic models, political policies, cultural and structural predispositions that would suggest plausible strategies for economic recovery and growth for both the elites and working class?

It is becoming abundantly clear that human capital as we've come to recognize it is becoming obsolete as the application of computers automates almost every facet of our lives. We have become so dependent upon automation and data management that we cannot buy even a single hamburger or train ticket when the computers are down. Cooking has not become a lost art, and other basic survival skills are purchased, instead of being individually mastered. Soon people will order their fast foods and other products from wristwatch sized voice activated computers, and pick up their products from the automated drive through dispensers, which may have a virtual human face on a computer screen.

Already, there are fewer tasks that computer automation can't do better and more cost-efficiently than humans. Over 80% of American workers are now employed in the service sector as manufacturing and programming jobs are outsourced to other nations with cheaper labor. Americans no longer make many things, but spend their time moving things around, repairing products made by foreigners, keeping track of data using programs and hardware produced overseas, and destroying their relations, communities and minds. This is not the correct formula for building and maintaining productivity and civility in a highly developed technological society, but is instead more descriptive of pre-industrial nations, minus trade skills.

Is America vulnerable to economic collapse and obsolescence? What steps can we take to protect ourselves and all Americans against the potential downfall of our civilization? Let's examine a plausible scenario based upon current
appearance of money-making vehicles to return exorbitant CEO compensation packages, to the detriment of both stockholders and employees.

Corporate profits are often not reinvested back into the domestic economy in the form of stockholder dividends, new hiring, and investment in buildings and equipment. Instead, profits are taken out of the U.S., and hidden in offshore tax-free havens, or invested overseas in nations with low standards of living with abundant cheap labor. How do irresponsible corporate actions contribute to strengthening the American economy? It doesn't, and instead, places America in potential economic peril.

How can our government protect us against such worse case scenarios? The recent federal efforts to stimulate the economy has had limited and sporadic success. Lowering the federal discount rate certainly has benefited banks and financial institutions, has encouraged home purchasing (but inflated home prices more than offsets lower mortgage interest rates) and loan refinancing, and has somewhat stimulated car purchasing, but it has not resulted in more jobs that would provide more spendable income for average Americans. The lower cost of borrowing money is not producing real gains because corporations and wealthy individuals are not reinvesting the surplus capital into the domestic economy, and continue to lay off thousands of workers as part of corporate strategy to enhance CEOs' stock options.

The tax cut, while well intentioned to provide more discretionary dollars to consumers is easily absorbed by runaway credit card debts and increased housing costs. The added $300-$600 tax break for most wage earners doesn't cover the added cost of consumer debt, as the tax cut is primarily transference of money from wage earners to creditors, lenders, and landlords. The most important issue previously missed by Greenspan and now by Bernanke, the currency czar is the continued loss of consumer confidence that results from a fear of job loss. As more workers lose confidence in the longevity of their jobs, they tend to abstain from making large purchases, and try to hang on to the little savings that they have for that stormy period that seems to linger on the horizon.

It's becoming urgent for the U.S. to develop economic targets that can be realistically achievable by the U.S. economy, against the larger backdrop of global competition. What economic policies could effectively turn around a sluggish economy while protecting its foundation against future peril and attacks? Firstly, we must develop a national vision of our economic future, set goals, and put into place national strategies to grow the economy while *protecting against* inflation, deflation, high unemployment, wild stock market speculation, higher budget deficit spending, and the transference of wealth to international conglomerates and speculators who have not qualms about robbing the life out of America for short-term gains.

We must not rely solely on tax cuts and lower interest rates to stimulate the economy because middle class consumers benefit relatively slightly, while the wealthy and corporate elites have not shown a desire to reinvest excess profits back into their commercial enterprises in America. Without placing substantial discretionary funds into the pockets of wage earners, coupled with increasing belief that the public will have jobs, consumers will hesitate to spend. Without added spending, economic activity remains sluggish and any systemic shock or external attacks against the economy would likely cause a slide into a significant recession, and possible economic depression.

America must become more independent of foreign trade to obtain manufactured goods. The U.S. must gain direct benefits from their occupation of Iraq's oilfields to stabilize oil prices. Agricultural products should be supported as a major source to balance our trade deficit, and to act as an anchor to ensure that our trading partners will continue to accept the U.S. dollar as payment for their imported goods. High tech industries, defense programs, biotechnologies, pharmaceuticals, and scientific research must be supported and freed from excessive red tape. These fields provide the foundation for future economic growth, protection against foreign competitors, and a safety margin against terrorism and conspiracies against the American economy, while improving the quality of life for current and future generations of Americans.

Immigration must be controlled, and all illegal foreign nationals must be identified, rounded up, and deported, which will decrease the demand for expensive infrastructure services by almost 10 million people. Saving vast amounts wasted on public spending for education, healthcare, social services, law enforcement, and incarceration of illegal immigrants would result in restoring local and state governments to solvency.

The public education system must be revamped and redesigned to provide the highly educated and trained professionals that are required by high tech, defense and scientific industries. We can no longer accept a broken public school system that produces the lowest performers among western nations. As long as our public school system continues to turn out students who are basically ignorant, lazy, and seekers of conveniences, we will continue to be trapped in an economy that depends on the purchase of services to compensate for mass stupidity. It is essential for mass media to take a more responsible path that contributes to improving society, rather than to encourage and exploit scandals, human conflict, and baser escapist drives for the sake of advertising dollars and commercial profits.

Television, movies, and computer games have become the media of destruction, where fun is equated to massive destruction, killing, profanity, and disregard for moral and responsible conduct. Our youth are being programmed into destroyers, who are able to delve inordinate hours in fantasy instead of spending time creating worthwhile things, pursuing constructive activities, or supporting their communities. This continuing trend is not healthy for a civilization that is becoming ever less civilized: absent a civil and educated citizenry who are capable of maintaining a complex high tech economy of the future; we will be doomed to suffer the consequences of our failures.

We need to minimize the adversarial relationships within our government. Much political conflict results from factions who spend inordinate time, energy, and expense to sabotage their competitors' legislative and political agendas. The drive for power, and to win at all cost invariable leads to a destructive course where personality innuendoes and not public issues become the fodder of the day. The supposed healthy public discourse rarely materializes, and instead is replaced by tidbits of media sound bites designed for the comprehension and consumption of fourth graders.

Democracy becomes muffled by rumors, misstatements, and media biases. There's a time for competition (hopefully without dirty tricks, slander, and scandals), but more often, there's more reason to invest time on finding cooperative common grounds for solving the people's problems. The people want answers and solutions, much more than the political squabbling and infighting that appear to absorb many of our government leaders. Give the people what they want, a stable and prosperous economy based upon a capitalist market system that is not corrupted by excessive greed, fraud and dishonesty. Our genius federal forefathers designed a political and economic system of the people, for the people, and by the people. Let's ensure that proper actions are taken to safeguard this great nation America against the economic perils of the present and future.

The basis for economic restoration lies in eight key factors that shape America's market-based economy: 1) restoring and maintaining public faith and trust in the American and global capitalistic market economic system; 2) enhancing anticipatory effects; 3) increasing investment in the economic infrastructure; 4) increasing discretionary consumer funds and savings; 5) decreasing unemployment fears and anxieties; 6) increasing net exports; 7) improving government efficiency; and 8) optimizing supply and demand equilibrium. Each factor requires specific remedies that can address economic woes in a reasonable systemic manner that reinforces stability, while improving certainty:

1. Restoring and maintaining public faith and trust in the American and global capitalistic market system through appropriate government regulations, protections and treaties.

   a) Markedly reduce corporate corruption and excessive executive compensation

   b) Regulate, audit and scrutinize corporate accounting practices

   c) Monitor and regulate monopolies and oligarchies to prevent price manipulation.

   d) Emphasize practice of organizational and executive ethical code of conduct

   e) Mandatory university classes on ethics, corruption, legal aspects of business

   f) Providing highly effective homeland security

   g) Rethinking "the ends justifies the means" paradigm to eliminate excessive greed

   h) Develop a clear political/economic/military/foreign relations vision and strategy

2. Enhancing anticipatory effects through accurate data collection and trend forecasting.

   a) Objective and factually based analysis, forecasting, rating, and transactions

   b) Realistic economic/employment outlook; lag effect, multipliers, equilibrium levels

   c) Applying technology and exploration for unlimited development of resources

   d) Intelligently managed distribution to minimize waste, and maximize conservation

3. Increasing investment in the economic infrastructure to increase GDP.

   a) Tax incentives for foreign investments in certain sectors of low employment

    b) Tax breaks for small businesses to reinvest and employ American workers

    c) Corporate tax breaks and subsidies for reinvesting in products and employment

    d) Tax incentives and subsidies for new technology and human capital development

4. Increasing discretionary consumer funds and savings.

    a) Full employment targets above subsistence pay rates (living wage)

    b) Control inflationary forces in housing, energy, banking, and insurance industries

    c) Tax breaks to strengthen specific segments of the economy suffering downturns

    d) Affordable housing and rents based upon assessment of community standards

    f) Low interest rate loans for consumer purchases and credit cards

    g) Development of new consumer-oriented industries and products

5. Decreasing unemployment fears and anxieties

    a) Job creation incentives to business sector

    b) Job training and retraining tax credits to individuals and employers

    c) Severance matching pay program for displaced employees

    d) Corporate health assessment of executive compensation & insurance rates

    e) Control the unjustified spiraling increases in the cost of insurance premiums

6. Increasing net exports and decreasing the international debt and balance of payments

    a) Decrease price in large quantity contracts for key exports; no tariff treaties

b) Track the amount of cash, stocks, bonds, and corporate assets owned by foreign nationals and governments; strategies to balance trade & assets

c) A strong dollar against the Euro and Japanese Yen

d) Enforce new rules on large amounts of cash redeemable per period

e) Control over international hedge funds investing in dollars

f) Improve relationships with international trade partners

7. Improving government efficiency through privatization and contracts

a) Centralized real time computerized tax collection with discount Incentives

b) Privatize certain segments of bureaucracy with adequate agency oversight

c) Improve bureaucratic effectiveness, efficiency and responsiveness through interdepartmental competition and incentives for cost-savings

8. Optimizing supply and demand equilibrium

a) Partnerships between government and universities to provide accurate and reliable economic analysis, projections, forecasting, and trend planning.

b) Computerized models on Internet to provide public with useful data & trends

c) Balancing distribution through integrated real time computer databases that identify supplies and demands by specific regions, towns, cities, and MSA's.

Improving America's economic infrastructure will permit Americans and the world to partake in vast new opportunities for development and controlled growth. The capitalistic market economy provides the ideal platform for realizing enormous wealth simply through satisfying human needs, desires, wants, and preferences. As political and social thought surpasses old outmoded and conflictual economic models spawned by the "zero-sum game" assumption, America and the entire human species will be able to harness the new global economic paradigm that awaits us on the event horizon.

A New Global Economic Paradigm

An economic paradigm shift is possible, where global economic prosperity is a goal within reach, as the rich become richer and the poor become middle-class. The economic wisdom of the past and present states that life is a "zero-sum game." This economic model suggests that there is a limit to resources, and conflict arises as a direct result of distribution hierarchies and processes that create great disparities among the world's populations. The wealthy global elites own and exploit world resources, as poverty envelops the majority of the world's population. It's a matter of history that the zero-sum economic model has created much turmoil, as civilizations conquered, plundered, and destroyed other cultures, only later to meet their own demise. As greed and the zero-sum game model interact, artificial shortages are created by those who hoard, to the detriment of those in greatest need. The zero-sum game of "greed versus need" has resulted in a world where the downtrodden and powerless are willing to fling their lives into destruction, with the hopes of destroying perceived symbols of the ruling class of wealthy elites.

A new economic paradigm that recognizes abundance must envelop the world order to eliminate the seemingly perpetual zero-sum game paradigm. We need not look too far to discover that life, our earth, and our universe is filled with limitless abundance! Certainly, there exist sufficient natural resources to support a reasonable human population of less than ten billion people, if resources are properly exploited and distributed. Management and distribution of world resources should eliminate waste, conserve the ecosystem, and intelligently use natural resources through technological enhancements to solve even the most persistent and perplexing human problems. The rich, who can provide capital and skills to optimize world resources, can become richer, as poverty is eliminated, and a growing global middle-class becomes the consumers of production that is owned by the wealthy elites. It's a win-win paradigm.

It is essential to examine the basic premise that created and perpetuates the zero-sum game mindset. During humans' earliest times, each day was a struggle for survival, as food, water and other usable natural resources appeared to be limited and in short supply, often requiring hoarding and defending. As civilizations and nations evolved from tribes and city-states, the fear of shortages continued, as human conflict, violence, and warfare sought to distribute the seemingly limited human resources to the powerful, creating a class of wealthy individuals. In today's world, nations struggle to protect their "national interests" as globalization of economic structures by multi-national corporations and the wealthy elites threaten to subjugate the economic interests and survivability of poorer nations. The zero-sum game continues to place large armies face to face across imaginary boundaries, waiting for the order to attack, destroy, kill, and plunder. Conflicts persist around the world; Korea, Iraq, Israel, Palestine, Liberia, just to name a few, with dozens more "hot spots" festering, waiting to be ignited by competition for the illusory limited wealth in the zero-sum game.

Getting beyond the illusion of limited natural resources, and recognizing the great abundance of untapped potential wealth will not be a simple task. Global coordination, vision, intelligent management, new technological applications, and sensible distribution of resources will be required to raise the global economic tide in a manner where the rich can get richer, as the poor become middle-class. Each continent and every nation possess natural wealth, some discovered and much unexplored, that can be transformed to wealth in the global marketplace. Africa, South America, Australia, Canada, India, China and Russia all contain vast undiscovered and unexplored stores of valuable minerals and other natural resources that can be transformed into wealth. Even in the West, a trip through America and Europe easily shows a vast bountiful landscape of unsettled areas, farmlands, pasture, and deserts that contain undiscovered and unexplored riches beyond its present day uses.

A global ten-point plan should be adopted by the United Nations to encourage the replacement of the conflict producing "zero-sum game" model with the realistic "abundance" paradigm. These ten points of development identify essential areas ripe for growth and wealth generation from crops, energy, minerals, recycling, and space by harnessing new technologies.

I.   Global Food Production
1.   Biotechnology to maximize harvests, control pests, disease and crop failures
2.   Improve crop rotation programs to restore land use without laying fallow
3.   Global computerization of farm production to eliminate duplication and waste
4.   Global computerized coordination of distribution and pricing
5.   New species of edible nutritious disease resistant crops r requiring less water

6. Genetically engineer new crops that can grow in the toughest terrains and soils

7. New farming techniques for harvesting the deserts, mountains, and marshlands

8. Use advantageous insects to increase harvest and control pests and disease

9. Use bacteria and microbes to increase harvest and control pests

10. Increase fisheries and oceanic seeding to replenish natural populations

11. Breed livestock, poultry and fish that grow faster, larger and healthier that can survive on a wider variety of cheaper grains, or foodstuffs not consumed by humans (e.g. weeds)

12. Genetically engineer heartier livestock and the feed it requires

13. Genetically engineer new breeds of livestock, poultry and fish for human consumption.

II. Global Food Distribution:

1. Food is sold and distributed to continental warehouses coordinated by management cooperatives, corporations, or government agencies, according to global treaties that establish specific protocols and procedures

2. Continental food banks distribute to member nations within its continental boundaries, and to private corporations in accordance to paid purchase agreements, credit/barter

3. UN food charity receives five percent of all food for redistribution to impoverished areas

4. Surplus food is sold to independent distributors for secondary and specialized markets

6.   Food prices are managed globally to derive incentive profit for distributors, predictable and steady income to producers, sufficient supplies and reasonable prices to consumers

III.   Oil and Gas Production, Pricing, and Distribution
1.   Predictable stability of world oil prices through graduated and structured 5-10 year guaranteed production and pricing levels by OPEC and other oil producing nations, with price increases capped at no greater than five percent above world growth levels.
2.   Global distribution equilibrium, with wealthier nations and consumers partially paying higher prices to subsidize poorer nations, on a temporary basis according to a global growth plan designed to raise the tide for all nations.
3.   Excessive retail profits limitation to prevent price gouging, fraud, corruption, and destructive levels of inflationary greed by middlemen, where any prices exceeding 100% retail mark-up must be redistributed 50% to the producer, 25% to government, with the remaining 25% to the retailers.

IV.   Mineral Exploration, Exploitation and Recycling:
1.   Existing mineral uses
        A.   Precious metals production should be stabilized to meet demand
        B.   New uses of existing supplies to enhance value of existing minerals & metals
2.   New uses from most abundant natural resources
        A.   Sand
        B.   Rock
        C.   Salt water

D. Kelp

E. Smog & air pollutants

F. Cow and animal wastes

G. Human waste products

H. Ocean floors

I. Lake and river sludge

J. Plankton

K. Bacteria and mold

L. Insects

3. Recycling

A. Automated mega-assortment recycling centers that process by the truckloads

B. Organic sumps reprocessing centers

V. Solar:

1. Energy for commercial buildings and homes

2. Energy to supplement vehicle hybrid engines

3. Satellite focused energy beams

4. More efficient solar collector arrays and solar cells

5. More efficient solar collector batteries

6. More efficient solar powered motors and engines

VI. Wind:

1. More efficient technologies, combining various solar blade designs in hybrid large and mini tower arrays

2. Compact designs for buildings and urban uses

3. Vehicle spoilers to convert wind velocity into battery power

VII. Lightening:

1. Balloon arrays

2. Discharge blimps

3. Electrical storage "lakes" – gigantic batteries

4. Lightening "farms"

VIII.   Hydro-electric:
1.   More efficient turbines at hydroelectric plants located in dams
2.   New technology offshore turbines to harness waves
3.   New technology turbines to harness strong river currents

IX.   New Materials:
1.   Lighter
2.   Stronger
3.   More flexible
4.   More resilient
5.   More esthetical
6.   Cheaper to produce
7.   Found in natural abundance
8.   New technological applications
9.   New markets created by consumers
10. Potential for expansive applications

X.   Space Exploration:
1.   Mine our moon and asteroids
2.   Mine Mars and Saturn's moons
3.   Explore and harness our solar system

Many of these ideas may appear to be radical, but none serves to threaten the existing economic hierarchical structure. In fact, several areas are currently under development by scientists, corporations and governments. Each area of development offers the wealthy elites vast opportunities to invest in greater profits, as the world's population benefits from the new technologies, materials, and global economic stability that will be spawned. The pursuit of abundance is natural and expansive. The fixation on the illusory zero-sum game model serves only to limit the production of wealth, as it casts billions into lives of poverty. Making the right choice for either progress or continued conflict will determine either the survival or extinction of humans, while generating a vast surplus of wealth for the global elites or fomenting destruction.

The pursuit of abundance will harness the great resources and technologies spent on military defense, and permit those investing in the next war instead to find greater purpose and power by investing in tomorrow's peaceful technologies based upon similar technologies now utilized for weapons design and production. Investing in abundance is "win-win" for everyone; the rich, poor, middle-class, the military, defense industries, high tech corporations, low tech companies, manufacturing sector, service sector, and governments of every nation on Earth. Nay-Sayers will always offer reasons why investing in abundance is impossible, but they'll be   left behind, clinging on to old outmoded models as if the Earth is the center of the universe.

Along with this new millennium, we must look to the future, as the methods of the past are behind us, and dragging them along only slows progress and burdens humanity as a whole.

The human species cannot afford to make extinction level mistakes due to shortsightedness. The focus of the "abundance paradigm" is to present an integrated and comprehensive economic policy that minimizes systemic shock, while maximizing economic gains to create a renewal cycle of economic growth and prosperity for all segments of the American populace. It is essential for America to build an economic infrastructure that will be strong enough to endure future competition and/or attacks from abroad. A future changed by a unified European economy, progressive Asian regionalism, development of South America and Africa, and more pervasive and efficient technologies presents America with both great opportunities and challenges to its global hegemony. Will a rising tide raise all ships in an expansive economic paradigm, or will the zero-sum game model continue to lock America and the rest of the global community in persistent conflicts and wars? What happens in global economics will have a direct bearing on whether human beings evolve to become efficient beneficiaries of resources found both on Earth and in our orbiting neighbors, or if our species become extinct from a global thermonuclear war. Our fates are in the hands of our best political and scientific minds. Let's all hope that our human best is going to be good enough.

GLOBALIZATION PARADIGM

How centralized global oligarchies will change the world order of the new world of tomorrow... for better or for worse, remains to be seen. Most people just want to have a job that can provide adequate income to meet their modest needs, to provide reasonable shelter, food, clothing, and a healthy environment for their families. However, the consolidation of economic power and assets among the elites has been greatly advanced by new technologies that allow them to gain the competitive edge, to position their multi-national corporations to manipulate supplies, labor and prices. The creativity of most individuals is being exploited in almost all fields of human endeavor, for the financial benefit of CEOs, overlords and the wealthy class.

Over the past ten years, the passages of historical international trade agreements have greatly increased redistribution of resources around the world. What have been the economic, political, and social effects of GATT, WTO and NAFTA, not to mention the next round of trade deals? Juxtaposed against supposed free trade treaties are the hidden hands of the IMF and World Bank, who often work in mysterious ways to enhance the control and economic power of the certain global elites.

What questions about globalization that must answered?

1. Where does the world stand now in the globalization trend?
2. Who and what groups are behind it?
3. Who stands to gain and who will lose?
4. Evolving geo-political pre-conditions and structural changes.
5. Is globalization good for humanity?
6. Globalization effects on despots, democracies and development.
7. How could globalization benefit everyone?

Let's discuss answers to these globalization trends and uncertainties.

1. *Where does the world stand now?*

There exist a general malaise among global governments to monitor and regulate the elites, monopolies, and oligarchies who are pushing to consolidate their control and wealth. Most government leaders and bureaucrats are generally lax in the enforcement of rules and laws that might limit centralization of wealth to elites, because the wealthy class can be formidable political allies or foes. Multi-national corporations (MNC's) are increasingly playing the "shell game" by moving manufacturing to transnational companies to benefit from cheap human capital.

Certain MNC's have essentially centralized global trade in various fields, and are building monopolies and oligarchies as they carve up the global pie, without regards to national interests or boundaries. Their goal is to control the price and supply of resources, production, distribution and markets on a global level to be able to dictate consumer prices from the cradle to the grave. Consequently, with centralized global oligarchies in control of supplies, they will be able to manipulate demand and prices to create artificial market conditions that do not conform to normal free market forces.

2. *Who and what groups are behind it?*

The corporate and government elites are essentially in bed with each other. Wealthy corporate executives make regular political contributions to political campaign war chests of those whose agenda is to do the bidding of the economic elites. After government officials have performed favors for the elites, they are assured lucrative retirement situations after leaving public service. Rumors abound regarding secret societies who enjoy access to top political and corporate leaders anywhere.

3. *Who stands to gain and who will lose?*

Centralize globalization will certainly benefit the globalizers, who are the corporate executives and government officials who benefit from controlling global prices. As usual, losers will be a mixed bag, depending on the geographical region, field, industry, and market demographics. While the employed will initially benefit from a broader range of products, increased availability, greater choices, and lower prices (due to cheap labor used in production), certain segments will lose jobs to cheaper labor markets, resulting in decreasing ability to buy products. As centralization of global trade and production is achieved by MNC's and oligarchies, supplies will be controlled and manipulated to drive down supplies, increase demand and profits to the greediest economic elites. As usual, the agents who represent MNC's and oligarchies, who broker all the major deals ranging from food to petroleum to weapons stand to consolidate their influence, wealth, and stature.

4. *Evolving structural changes and pre-conditions.* Globalization requires the cooperation of world governments, who see short-ranged economic benefits to be derived from employment, investments, and personal financial benefits. As their domestic economies become more productive, and the living standards of their people rise, governments see greater political stability and longevity. However, many do not realize that they are consenting to a roller coaster ride that is likely to come crashing off track. For example, NAFTA had initially been highly beneficial to Mexico, a major U.S. trade partner. Many MNC's relocated entire segments of assembly, manufacturing, and production to Mexico, until they discovered cheaper labor and deals in China and India. Consequently, natural inflation that was caused by higher wages and purchasing power also caused prices to rise during times of high employment. The long-term problem arose when jobs vanished to overseas, and along with them the jobs that produced national and regional income; however, the higher prices remained beyond the means of the unemployed and underemployed, while prior to globalization, local economies were generally self-sufficient.

5. *Is globalization good for humanity?*

Certain aspects of free global trade are useful in equalizing the distribution of resources, which benefit all economic classes. The transnational cooperation between the business and government sectors translates to greater communication, diplomacy, understanding, and tolerance of differences. The exposure of entire societies and peoples to foreign products, cultures, and ideas creates greater tolerance and acceptance of diversity, which becomes a foundation for global peace. That's the upside. On the downside is the tendency of MNC's, oligarchies, elitist corporate executives and the world's wealth to become defocused from humanitarian and environmental concerns and issues. Their profit strategies do not depend on social responsibility, and if the potential consequences of their economic agendas result in harming and destroying cultures, jobs, local autonomy, and the environment, then they feel the ends justifies the means. They legitimize their actions by pointing to the Darwin paradigm of survival of the fittest, justifying a notion that the weak do not deserve to survive, and therefore they shouldn't. Of course, they don't mention the obvious fact that their wealth gives them a thousand fold advantage over everyone else, and permits them to garnish a level of economic power that can potentially be used to extort the governments of the world to do their bidding.

6. *Effects on despots, democracies and development.*

It is unclear whether globalization will most benefit democratic civilizations with relatively free and competitive markets, or despotic systems controlled by oligarchies, or eventually lead to the ruination of the entire world economy and nation-states as a result of the rise of centralized global oligarchies. It is likely each scenario will have its day during global evolution, and be profoundly affected by advanced computer technology. Biblical prophecy may be fulfilled when people won't be able to buy or sell without the "mark of the beast." which may turn out to be a sub dermal GPS micro data chip. Let's hope not.

7.   *How could globalization benefit everyone?*
In theory, if free markets were left to function without unfair intervention or regulation by governments, monopolies, and oligarchies, natural supply and demand forces would cause an equilibrium price that would satisfy consumer needs. In the real world, the uneven distribution of resources and supplies due to corporate manipulation cause drastic fluctuations in world prices. The major deal makers and brokers who are the hubs, middlemen, and gatekeepers of the global economy are only interested in their commissions and profits, and are not concerned about humanitarian issues. In theory, we could live in a world where every global citizen enjoys a living wage that provides them the ability to participate in the global economy, and consequently, distribution would become broader, making products widely available and beneficial to all people. The reality is globalization exploits seeks to exploit the cheapest labor pools, which creates a dynamic and unpredictable future for humans trying to survive on low wages.

World leaders need to constructively discuss and review accelerated developments in the globalization game. Oligarchies often do not have social responsibility and humanitarianism as part of their greed paradigm. The pre-conditions, pros and cons, probable scenarios, consequences, and outcomes of centralized global trade need to be thoroughly explored. Objective research needs to identify who (and which groups) stand to benefit the most economically and politically from globalization. What are certain structural changes that will signal the onset and configuration of centralized globalization that is not too far off in our developing future? Let's discuss the facts and evaluate current geo-political economic issues and trends that must be addressed by world leaders.

1. *Evaluation of current degree and breadth of globalization.*
    a. Accurate data and statistics is urgently needed to allow policy makers to understand global market movements.
    b. A clear picture of global product production and regional distribution must be developed to determine what groups are benefiting or being hurt by globalization, both short-term and long-term effects.
    c. Consolidation of market share by large holding Companies
    d. MNC's, oligarchies, and corporations needs to be tracked and monitored to determine profit profiles, and whether centralization of economic control benefits people more than it displaces or hurts people, workers, and consumers.
2. *MNC's, elites, trade brokers, governments, secret international organizations), NGO's, and global oligarchies (i.e. diamonds).*

Imagine living in a future era where MNC's, economic and political elites, and oligarchies control the supply and prices of everything. Would these powerful segments voluntarily lower prices to levels that would benefit workers and the poor? Or

would they likely manipulate prices to obtain greater profits?
We already live in a world where one percent of the world's
population owns and/or controls over 60 percent of the world's
assets, and the top ten percent controls over 90 percent, leaving
the rest of the world's ninety percent to fight over the remaining
ten percent. Is there something wrong with this picture? Will
this greed paradigm ever stop? What type of world will it be if a
dozen individuals were someday able to gain control the top
twelve industries in the world, then have the power to set prices
for food, electrical power, computers, gasoline, gold, military
hardware, automobiles, housing, clothing, insurance rates, credit
cards, and bank interest on savings and loans? What type of
world would that likely be for consumers?

3.   *The elites versus the poor.*
     The history of mankind has always been a struggle of the
     poor to survive the dictates and whims of the powerful and
     wealthy. The elites benefit from the labor of the masses.
     In the not so distant past, they were slave owners and
     industrialists who put children to work in the mines,
     factories and farms, and forced long hours and extremely
     poor work conditions on the masses. Today's elites
     downsize their corporations and outsource jobs
     to create more profit for their CEOs and Board Chairmen,
     as they shop the world for regions of trainable cheap
     labor. The working class is viewed as consumers, whose
     life purpose by default is to work for the rich, to make the
     rich even wealthier through the hard labor and
     consumption of workers. In fact, the elites have
     used the schools, churches, and media to socialize the
     masses into believing the so call "hard work ethic"

is a good thing, and those workers who are highly productive are models of good citizens. As elitists convince everyone to work harder, CEOs and their non-working buddies head for the golf course, their yachts, and mansions to be waited upon by hard working people. The elites are generally a lazy bunch of demanding, spoiled and dictatorial manipulators. They see other people as tools to the fulfillment of their every need. Most elitists, beyond having wealth, are a bunch of untalented, uninspiring, and narrow-minded people who are incapable of doing very much for themselves.

Most elitists have gained their wealth through four ways; inheritance, lucky investments, trickery, or crime. None of these methods require hard work or practical skills; consequently, they know nothing about working hard and don't want to work hard. Working hard is for their employees whose life purpose is to serve. Being served is the paradigm of the elites, who are owners of property and people, and consequently feel entitled to rule and be served by commoners. It is highly unlikely this relationship between the rich and poor will ever change, not as long as social values are skewed to boost up the elites, and to devalue the downtrodden.

4.   *Economic, political, cultural, religious, and environmental impact of globalization.*

      a.   The economic impact on the short-term basis is to spread jobs around the world, which boosts regional economies while increasing profits to the elites. The long-term impact is uncertain, as economic development has a history of cyclical changes, and most industries have experienced the periods of boom, and the devastation of burst and bust.

b. The political effects of globalization is to place bureaucrats, gatekeepers, and government officials in a "money-mania" position. Special interest lobbyists, who usually represent the elites, temp and corrupt public officials with various enticements behind closed doors. As the wealth of elites magnify, their economic and political influence expands, as they corrupt government policy makers who partake in the supper of crows and drink from the well of deceit.

c. Cultural information will become intermixed due to greater availability and interaction of westernized products and values to local indigenous cultures. History has shown that the demise and ruination of world cultures soon follow the advent of modern materialism, gadgets, clothing, and the values of consumerism.

d. Religious values tend to reflect the leadership of religious organizations, whose spiritual rulers either enforce or relax strict religious codes. History illustrates that where there is wealth and materialism, fundamental religious values are interpreted to promote an acceptance of consumerism. In poorer nations and regions, a stricter interpretation of religious values is promoted to discourage materialism. As globalization continues to spread consumerism and desire for material wealth, religion will fall or be pushed aside in its path. The rise of religion appeared during eras when most people were poor, struggling and destitute. Religion gave them hope for a pleasant afterlife, so they could endure their misery in this life. As the distribution and control of natural resources, money and materialism are becoming a global phenomenon, people who are able to enjoy the material benefits of consumerism will normally relax their religious fervor, and interpret their dogma to permit greater enjoyment of worldly goods. They need look no farther than the examples that their religious leaders will demonstrate, who enjoy the materialism and comforts that collection plates provide to their religious organizations, ministers, rabbis, mullahs, priests, swamis, and gurus. Let's face reality: when there's no money around, people do without, then rationalize that the pursuit of materialism is unessential for enlightenment and happiness, and to see the pursuit of money as being an evil influence. However, when there is money available to be gotten, people justify its pursuit by saying money is good, it's only when it is spent on immoral activities that money becomes bad.

e. Globalization means global trade and the exploitation of global resources; both raw materials and labor. The world has witnessed increased development that is beginning to show detrimental effects on global environments through deforestation, air and water pollution, global warming, species extinction, erosion, depletion of fisheries, ozone depletion, and accelerated melting of the ice caps. These trends will continue unabated, as the population explosion and consequential impact for more development, industry, food, water, living space will seriously erode the natural environment, possibly to a point of no return.

5. *Efficient and effective global distribution versus hoarding and exploitation.*

    a.   In theory, there exist sufficient wealth and resources in the world to cloth, shelter, feed, and employ everyone. It is only because one percent of humans own 60%, and another 9% of people own 30% of everything, that the remaining 90% of the Earth's inhabitants must spread the remaining 10% of the world's resources around. The U.S., which comprises 6% of the world's population consume over 30% of its resources, and contribute at least 40% of the world's environmental pollution.

    b.   As developing nations increase their wealth due to benefits of globalization, coupled with inevitable population gains, the environmental pressure will become detrimental to both nature and humans. Long before world population reaches 300 billion people (which is estimated as the upper most limit that natural rainfall could support), environmental degradation will probably make life unbearable. The hoarding of wealth and abuse of world resources by the elites, coupled with ignorant and destructive activities of development, within the context of an exploding world population can only spell a disaster of great magnitude, just waiting to happen. It's not a matter of "if", it's just a matter of "when." Elites must realize that destroying the environment hurts not only the masses, but themselves.

6. *New World Order, the UN, diplomacy, world vision, and the ultimate military options.*

    a.   The world may be going through another cycle, perhaps the final cycle of imperialism, under the guise of globalization. The spoils of the world will likely come under the control of a global network of the ultra-wealthy, each carving up world resources, industries, and populations through their oligarchies, and monopolies.

    b.   The United Nations will become the public hand that serves the wishes of the economic war lords, who will control key politicians and generals in the major governments of the world. Diplomacy will become the euphemistic term for bribery, as greedy officials will succumb to "offers one can not refuse" offered by the elites, otherwise they become defeated or recalled by the media-manipulated electorate.

    c.   The mantra for ambitious and/or greedy Alpha (type A) people in both the business and public sector will be "Serve the elites to be an elite." Their common vision will be to control and manage the world's resources, assets, wealth and people by applying a cost-efficient business model, utilizing super computers to provide real time meta data required to coordinate global markets.

e.   Those governments and people who resist and rebel against the elitist global paradigm will be hunted down by the world's integrated military, intelligence and policing agencies.

The war on terrorism will be refocused to eliminate resistance to the economic interests of the world's elites, whenever, wherever, and however it may occur. A shakedown of terrorist groups, and states who support them will result in subsequent wars to remove anti-globalization leaders. The resultant world order will provide a stable and relatively peaceful environment for nations who *are essentially owned by the global elites.*

7.   *Can centralized globalization or alternative global paradigms present realistic opportunities to build an ideal world* where happiness, peace, and global cooperation can be a reality?

a.   Poorer nations are usually ruled by autocratic despots or divided among regional warlords, with varying degrees of loyalty to a distant central government. Globalization is likely to solidify the power of tyrants because global free trade is not predicated on a humane rational system of national governance among its participants. Where MNC's and oligarchies invest in harvesting natural resources from non-democratic countries, the increased wealth will permit despots to purchase modern armaments, and even to obtain WMDs through illegal arms merchants.

b.   Among westernized nations, the majority of its population feel they have an opportunity through hard work, ability, and determination to become middle-class, or even rich. The middle class believes in notions of pursuing happiness, and generally view money as one means toward gaining greater freedom and happiness. On the other hand, most economic elites pursue money as wealth building goals that confirm their superior status and social value. Somewhere there is a nexus between money and the pursuit of personal freedoms and happiness. Perhaps, there is a minimal level of money required to produce and sustain a minimal level of happiness; and a maximum level of satisfaction at which no additional wealth can increase further happiness.

How will the rapidly evolving global changes affect average people in present times, and in the next 5-10 years? Here's some questions, the answers which should clarify who will likely benefit, and who will likely suffer from the effects of globalization.

1.   *Who are the global elites?*

Some are listed in the Forbes 100, but it is unlikely that the *true elites* would want their names known by the general public, which would potentially make them and their families the targets of terrorists, criminals, and psychopaths. Can you blame them? The *true global elites* most likely influence or manipulate world leaders surreptitiously, hidden from public view or news headlines. Corporate elites, such as the Walton's of Wal-Mart, and Gates of Microsoft are non-political, as evidenced by their lack of immunity from public and government scrutiny. The *true elites* never attract that type of attention, as scrutiny is an impediment to manipulation and financial advantages.

2. *Who are the global power-brokers?*

    Eliminate the despots who comprise "the Axis of Evil" because they rule relatively poor nations and have little economic or international political clout. Look to the "old money" that has been around since kingdoms and empires existed, which remains in the hands of royal families and their descendants; also quiet heirs of great industrialists and tycoons, corporate executives of MNCs, holding companies, monopolies, oligarchies, and Fortune 100 companies who are not in the public light. The heads of elected governments are not always the real powerbrokers, but often times represent the agendas of the powerful and wealthy who helped to finance the campaigns which placed them in office.

3. *What industries and global resources do these elites control? (go to littlesis.org)*

    The obvious ones are diamonds, gold, other precious gems and metals, strategic minerals used in manufacturing computers and military weaponry. In addition, corporate farms, pharmaceuticals, the military-industrial complex, global shipping, real estate tycoons and re-insurers. Mass media, publications, multi-national auto manufacturers, banking, and commodities traders. There are many other areas that the elites collectively control, where small businesses are able to service their "after-markets."

4.   *How do elites see the role of human beings, in terms of self-determination?*

Let's face it, if the global elites could have their way, they would probably want a return to slavery, indentured servitude, serfdom, and sweat shops. The historical paradigm of the wealthy class has always been the exploitation of labor. The economic elites believe they are superior to the faceless masses, and feel they are born into this world with an entitlement, or have earned the entitlement to be served, respected and admired by the working class. It is beneath their dignity to mingle with the poor, unless they gain social status by providing a tax-deductible building, property, or university endowment to the public, which is then named after them to acknowledge and celebrate their high status. Someday, robotics and artificial intelligence will be possible, or genetically engineered humanoids will be common. Subsequently, billions of human beings will become obsolete, and labor exploitation will be a thing of the past. In the likely ensuing scenario, the usefulness of the poor and working class will become questionable, and new "herd trimming" strategies may be employed to control or reduce population growth. The elites feel most people are just wasting space and global resources, causing pollution and crowding out the most pristine natural environments, which they would love to own for themselves and their families.

5.   *How will technological advances and applications enable theseglobal elites to gain greater control?*

The future pervasiveness of computer technology, microchips, genetically modified foods, genetically engineered animals and human beings, portable robotics, and nano-technology will certainly enable the elites to gain greater control of human and corporate assets in manipulated markets. People will become managed consumers, whose survival options will be limited by social, economic and legal structures installed by the elites.

6. *How will labor migration affect the future economic and political map of the world?*

    Several dynamic labor migration cycles will follow, one after another, depending upon technological advances and markets that may be created. The poor will always migrate toward job markets, as global urbanization has historically been the trend that replaced rural farming. In the current cycle, computer and new technologies have moved jobs to low salary labor markets abroad. National boundaries will not need to be traversed by immigrants, as certain jobs will exploit international labor and other commodities and products will be sought from low cost regions, temporarily benefiting developing nations, often to the detriment of developed job markets. Eventually, after global and political stability is attained, freer movement of nationals to the source of jobs may be possible, but until then, unemployment will increase in developed nations, unless new technology provides new employment opportunities to displaced workers.

7. *What shrinking options will be available for the laborers andconsumers in the global economy?*

    Workers will be forced to obtain more specific training, education, and skills that are in demand by new technology. As education becomes available via on-line education programs, or simply off the Internet, worker advancement and employability will greatly depend on personal improvement. On the other hand, those who are able to achieve higher paying positions, or who benefit from business ownership, and the economic elites will be able to hire low-tech workers to do those things that they don't care to do. There will only be two types of jobs, highly skilled technology jobs, and low-tech service jobs. Everything else will be done by computer-driven automatic or robotic systems, including retail, fast foods, court system, tax collection, accounting, auditing, medical diagnosis, drug dispensing, and many service careers.

7. *Will people be able to "opt out" to alternative economies, or will the New World Order prevent it?*

What will people be able to "opt out" to? Some may opt to buy small plots of land, and attempt to live off the land. Others may elect to live under modified commune or collective arrangements. Small local trade economies may develop in the business of resale of used or secondary market products. But the vast majority of consumers will undoubtedly opt for inclusion in the convenient and efficient computer automated robotic systems of distribution. Few urbanites are prepared to leave the conveniences of urban life, to regress a hundred years into the past to struggle with uncertainty and hard work that is part and parcel to living off the land. It is unlikely people will be forced by government, whether local or global, to partake in the matrix of the new world economic order; it won't be necessary, as people will flock to accept the subdermal all knowing GPS computer chip implant to be able to buy and sell.

9. *Will economic dominance permit small groups of elites to dictate global political and social policies?*

If one hundred people were given the choice to become part of the global elite, versus remaining an anonymous powerless and insignificant worker, it is highly unlikely more than ten percent would honestly choose to remain relatively powerless and poor. It's not so much who is in the elitist position, but a matter of the philosophical orientation of elitists, how they justify their high positions, and the means that they use to maintain their entitlements. Unfortunately, given the opportunity, the poor would likely be just as voracious, insensitive, selfish, and self-serving as the rich, if only they could obtain the chance. What we need is for more members of the elites to demonstrate greater social responsibility, especially if their wealth depends on the exploitation of laborers, who are also consumers of the products that provide huge profits to the elites.

Globalization and free trade continues to proceed, spread, and entice the governments, workers, and elites of the world, as all partake in the benefits of a wider redistribution of employment and wealth. The elites are certain to increase their assets, and as regions of development materialize, the sea of prosperity will also rise for the formerly poor. The hidden danger arises from imbalances and cycles that may arise, with potential sudden reversals of fortunes for low-paid workers, as the elites shop for cheaper global labor markets. There are no guarantees, and the long-term benefits and costs of globalization remains to be seen and is uncertain.

Corporate Marketing Ethics Paradigm

Marketing is the public face of companies and businesses that engage in commerce with the public at large, government agencies and other businesses. On page 32 of the textbook, MKTG, an information box entitled *What's Expected of Marketers* delineates the general principles, norms and values as ethical marketing standards:

Norms:

- Marketers must first do no harm
- Marketers must foster trust in the marketing system
- Marketers should embrace, communicate, and practice the fundamental ethical values that will improve consumer confidence in the integrity of the marketing exchange system

Ethical Values:

- Honesty
- Responsibility
- Fairness
- Respect
- Openness
- Citizenship

While these standards sound good and approximately one-third of corporations have adopted some internal ethical standards, we often find marketing deception is the rule of the day. Let's look at these ethical marketing ideals to see if the largest recipient of TARP loans from the federal government, Goldman Sachs who also benefited from the AIG bailout, has satisfied their corporate code of conduct. The publicly stated Goldman's Ethics Policy is: "Integrity & Honesty Are at The Heart of Our ... Goldman Sachs" [1]

How well does Goldman Sachs measure up to the ethical norms of marketing?

1. *Marketers must first do no harm* is a noble ideal, however recent disclosures by the SEC in its lawsuit against Goldman Sachs alleges that the company and its executives conspired with a major hedge fund to intentionally swindle the public and investors who bought sub-prime loan based securities.

2. *Marketers must foster trust in the marketing system* is not the fundamental result of the example set by a greedy and corrupt system operating on Wall Street where stock prices in certain companies real and fraudulent are marketed by stock brokers and advisers as solid investments when in fact insider information shows the high ratings afforded by the 3 largest corporate stock rating services are excessively manipulated to present investors with bullish market projections.

3. Marketers should embrace, communicate, and practice the fundamental ethical values that will improve consumer confidence in the integrity of the marketing exchange system. Again, the conspiracy of Goldman Sachs executives with hedge fund executives, government regulators (past Dept. of Treasury Hank Paulsen who was past-CEO of Goldman Sachs before "stepping down" to assume the federal regulatory role), and stock rating bureaus such as A.M. Best and Standard and Poor has served to leave the public high and dry... broke and bankrupt.

It has been disclosed that there existed "near-constant phone contact between then-Treasury Secretary Henry Paulson and his successor as Goldman Sachs CEO, Lloyd Blankfein, during the height of the financial crisis last September... the Treasury Department Paulson's ethics agreement, in which he pledged not to participate in matters involving Goldman Sachs, and the waiver to that agreement granted by White House counsel Fred Fielding."

Furthermore, "Of the dozens of phone calls between Paulson and Blankfein, 26 occurred before Paulson requested and obtained a waiver to deal with matters relating to Goldman Sachs... [it was on] the morning of Sept. 17, a day after the AIG bailout, which ultimately handed Goldman $13 billion of taxpayers' money -- before Paulson obtained the ethics waiver... While selling his stock in Goldman, Paulson kept his Goldman pension benefits when he became Treasury Secretary." [2]

Clearly the greatest beneficiary of the emergency federal bailout known as TARP I that then Secretary of the Treasury Hank Paulsen personally pushed through Congress benefited his prior-employer Goldman Sachs who was guarantor of his sizable retirement pension. This cozy relationship between Goldman Sachs who was once marketed as the "gold standard" of investment banking clearly demonstrates widespread disregard and violation of ethical and business standards.

Ethical Values:

1   *Honesty* – Goldman Sachs fell far short of the practice of corporate or executive integrity when they "cheated" investors

2   *Responsibility* - Goldman Sachs' deceptive actions and dishonest investment policies clearly showed no acceptance of fiduciary responsibility to its investors, employees, or to the general public

3   *Fairness* – Goldman Sachs' conspiracy to sell investment securities in order to accumulate public capital in dubious investments, then utilize a major hedge fund to attack the securities was predatory and destructive of the financial interests of all investors, whether individual 401k retirement funds, employee pension funds, insurance trusts or public bank deposits.

4.   *Respect* – Goldman Sachs' executive emails clearly demonstrate a total disregard and disdain for public investors as their desire for profit by any means resulted in deliberate actions to short investors by betting against the very securities they marketed as solid deals.

5   *Openness* – Goldman Sachs' secret dealings surrounding its securities marketing were backroom conspiracies between their executives, government regulators and executives from hedge funds and credit/stock rating services where transparency was the last desirable consideration as openness would have certainly exposed their diabolical plots.

6   *Citizenship* – Goldman Sachs' key role in contributing to the near collapse of the American economy is almost treasonous. We Americans worry about external terrorist attacks and threats against our property, but when multi-national American conglomerates like Goldman Sachs attack our economic property and assets, their executives receive exorbitant executive bonuses and a chiding by Congress while they literally stole money out of the pockets of retirees and pension funds. No one who conspired to accomplish these dastardly economic deeds of ill gotten wealth goes to jail for costing investors over $1 billion in lost wealth [3] while a petty thief would face the judge for stealing a piece of bread were he hungry.

In conclusion, while the talk of corporate ethics is the flavor of the day, the practice of business ethics on Walls Street by some of the world's largest investment banks (i.e. Goldman Sachs), insurance companies (AIG), oil companies (Enron) clearly shows the so-called corporate ethical standards are more marketed for public consumption as the illusion of ethical conduct to encourage public investment than evidenced by its practice.

A NEW GLOBAL ECONOMIC PARADIGM

An economic paradigm shift is possible, where global economic prosperity is a goal within reach, as the rich become richer and the poor become middle-class. The economic wisdom of the past and present states that life is a "zero-sum game." This economic model suggests that there is a limit to resources, and conflict arises as a direct result of distribution hierarchies and processes that create great disparities among the world's populations. The wealthy global elites own and exploit world resources, as poverty envelops the majority of the world's population. It's a matter of history that the zero-sum economic model has created much turmoil, as civilizations conquered, plundered, and destroyed other cultures, only later to meet their own demise. As greed and the zero-sum game model interact, artificial shortages are created by those who hoard, to the detriment of those in greatest need. The zero-sum game of "greed versus need" has resulted in a world where the downtrodden and powerless are willing to fling their lives into destruction, with the hopes of destroying perceived symbols of the ruling class of wealthy elites.

A new economic paradigm that recognizes abundance must envelop the world order to eliminate the seemingly perpetual zero-sum game paradigm. We need not look too far to discover that life, our earth, and our universe is filled with limitless abundance! Certainly, there exist sufficient natural resources to support a reasonable human population of less than ten billion people, if resources are properly exploited and distributed. Management and distribution of world resources should eliminate waste, conserve the ecosystem, and intelligently use natural resources through technological enhancements to solve even the most persistent and perplexing human problems. The rich, who can provide capital and skills to optimize world resources, can become richer, as poverty is eliminated, and a growing global middle-class becomes the consumers of production that is owned by the wealthy elites. It's a win-win paradigm.

It is essential to examine the basic premise that created and perpetuates the zero-sum game mindset. During humans earliest times, each day was a struggle for survival, as food, water and other usable natural resources appeared to be limited and in short supply, often requiring hoarding and defending. As civilizations and nations evolved from tribes and city-states, the fear of shortages continued, as human conflict, violence, and warfare sought to distribute the seemingly limited human resources to the powerful, creating a class of wealthy individuals. In today's world, nations struggle to protect their "national interests" as globalization of economic structures by multi-national corporations and the wealthy elites threaten to subjugate the economic interests and survivability of poorer nations. The zero-sum game continues to place large armies face to face across imaginary boundaries, waiting for the order to attack, destroy, kill, and plunder. Conflicts persist around the world; Korea, Iraq, Israel, Palestine, Liberia, just to name a few, with dozens more "hot spots" festering, waiting to be ignited by competition for limited illusory wealth in a zero-sum game.

Getting beyond the illusion of limited natural resources, and recognizing the great abundance of untapped potential wealth will not be a simple task. Global coordination, intelligent management, new technological applications, and sensible distribution of resources will be required to raise the global economic tide in a manner where the rich can get richer, as the poor become middle-class. Each continent and every nation possess natural wealth, some discovered and much unexplored that can be transformed into wealth in the global marketplace. Africa, South

America, Australia, Canada, India, China and Russia all contain vast undiscovered and unexplored stores of valuable minerals and other natural resources that can be transformed into wealth. Even in the West, a trip through America and Europe easily
shows a vast landscape of unsettled areas, farmlands, pasture, and deserts that contain undiscovered and unexplored riches beyond its present uses.

President George W. Bush's new space initiative is a bold step toward human evolution, because the scientific discoveries that can occur will have beneficial technological and economic results. Mankind's expansion of knowledge of our solar system and beyond will concurrently provide us with profound insights to our own make-up and possible purpose in God's great universal realm. Great advances in bio-technology, genetic engineering, nano-technology, computer micro and nano-processes, development of new materials, advanced avionics and rocketry, biometrics, space medicine, and untold new fields will emerge from our nation's united effort to push our earthly envelop into near space and beyond, where no man has yet to stand.

We need visionary leadership and idealism to build a better and more humane and civil world. Difficult decisions were made to depose Saddam, to free Iraq, and to protect our homeland. A futuristic and pro-active approach toward problem solving will greatly enhance human progress toward world peace and economic progress, while keeping America and Americans at the forefront of positive human endeavors. Americans have always had a penchant and spirit for development, discovery, exploration, entrepreneurial, and scientific and humanitarian progress. Humans may not self-destruct after all if we focus on building rather than destroying (let's also take adequate redundant precautions to decontaminate and isolate new materials retrieved from space, to prevent world wide infection by unknown viruses, bacteria, or other yet undiscovered but potentially lethal life forms).

References for Corporate Marketing Ethics:

[1] Retrieved from the World Wide Web on May 18, 2010 from www.vault.com/wps/portal/usa/blogs/entry-detail/?blog_id...

[2] Elliott, Justin, *Interesting Reading: Paulson's '06 Ethics Agreement And '08 Goldman Waive* - August 10, 2009. Retrieved from the World Wide Web on May 18, 2010 from tpmmuckraker.talkingpointsmemo.com/.../08/interesting_reading_paulsons _ 06_ethics_agreement_a.php

[3] *Update: SEC says Goldman defrauded investors of $1 billion | Raw Story Apr 16, 2010 ... A fair trial OPEN TO THE PUBLIC, that lost ALL of their money. ... GOLDMAN SACHS EAGER TO PAY 100 MILLION DOLLAR FINE ON 1 BILLION DOLLAR ...* Retrieved from the World Wide Web on May 18, 2010 from rawstory.com/rs/2010/0416/charges-goldman-sachs-fraud/

TECHNOLOGY AND ECONOMICS PARADIGM

Miniaturization of communications technology is revolutionizing the methods of consumer behavior where Google Glass and smart phones is making shopping and banking into a personally convenient activity. Following is a fictitious visualization of how technology is rapidly changing our economic landscape.

Bijohn is a French foreign exchange student in the U.S. who wears on his wrist a mini-computer that permits him to see his "account info" and responds to him via verbal commands and responses directly to his "Blue Tooth" earpiece. Bijohn jumps into his eight year old Citroen and complains to himself, "there has to be a better way to get around than this ancient piece of junk". As he drives by a car dealership on his home, he complains on his watch-phone to a salesperson who he waves to, stating that he can't shop from his car like most people in the 21st century, and as soon as he could save enough money, he'll buy a new BMW Global Cruiser with the automatic radar activated accident avoidance system, in-vehicle e-shopping, and voice activated entertainment system.

The auto salesman responds that he'll email the information on the new car to the caller ID number of Bijohn's mini-computer with a promotional savings plan that will finance and reserve the car of Bijohn's dreams, today. An advanced order may be placed with the manufacturer either in Japan, the U.S., Ghana or Mexico, depending on shipping cost as adjusted by current monetary exchange rates. Bijohn says he'll check it out later, and both say good-bye.

When Bijohn gets home, things are better. He's completely wired, and gets comfortable as soon as he walks through the front door. People still have to walk, but rarely to work or school. He commands his resident computer to "find mom" and the

satellite tracking system responds "mom is in car, state id number 7TGOTO8T, going east on I-10 at 70 mph, crossing I-15 juncture". He commands, "talk" and "see" and his mom comes on his 70 inch flat DVD-HD-TV picture hanging entertainment center. "Hi mom." "Hi Son!" "Uhh... do you think you can email me more credits into my account? My car's a drag and I can get a special on a new car." "Well, Hun, let me talk to your father first, okay?" "I gotta get my hair done, so I'll talk to you later Sweetie." "Okay, mom... see ya." "Bye."

Some things change, and some things seem to stay the same, only at another level. Within five years, and certainly by the end of this new decade, the wedding of computer, communications and technology will become far-reaching and will affect most aspects of individual lives in our global economic village. Technological advances already permit the following scenario in reality; however until individual financial investment in the new technologies catch up with the science to warrant mass production of existing prototypes, the world will not rapidly benefit from global e-commerce.

Consider the following afternoon in the life of a typical consumer in the year 2020 where Bijohn, a third year college student is listening to his college professor's web-broadcasted lecture on the "requisite aspects of designing consumer friendly web pages" on his interactive wristwatch HDTV mini-computer. He vocally responds to the professor's questions and receives instantaneous feedback on his answers. Several academicians collaborated on the curriculum of this class according to their areas of expertise, consequently, Bijohn may choose by voice command which teacher he wishes to query about particular subject areas. He is instantaneously connected to the respective professor's web page which gives various options, interacting to answer students' questions. Bijohn commands, "see" and his teaching assistant assigned to professor "X" sees and advises him on a solution. Bijohn plans to call the professor back during his normal office hours and tells his watch to call for an appointment, and when confirmed, to automatically connect him at that time. He downloads his homework using his HDTV mini wrist-top computer.

A call comes in on Bijohn's watch from France and the caller speaks in French, then Bijohn commands, "hear" and the conversation is translated to him in English. He commands "see" and the other party responds "ok" and they are in full audio-visual mode. Another incoming call appears on his wrist computer, identifying the caller. He responds "see-too" and the screen splits, showing the other caller. As it happens, the other caller is from Japan, so Bijohn commands "hear-too". Since both callers know Bijohn and have talked to each other before, he tells them that he is simultaneously talking to both of them and commands "meet" and now they are all connected, seeing each other and hearing the other's voice translated with similar tonal qualities, pitch, and articulation in real time.

After a brief conversation, Bijohn stays on with his friend from Japan because he want to play the latest virtual reality fighting game that is hitting the global market. His Japanese friend and Bijohn put on portable "VR" glasses with built-in headsets and plug in the electrical stimulation module that runs from four electrodes that are plugged into the mini wrist-top that picks up movement from the sensors strapped around his ankles and from his "fighting gloves". They are able to fight in real time because the resident program is contained in a satellite that utilizes lasers to bridge two connecting satellites that utilize microwave transmission. They both look forward to the globalization of fiber optics within the next decade so they could fight each other at the speed of light from their remote locations.

Bijohn thinks the game is great and commands "shop-three" and his mini palm tells him the prices, shipping cost and time and warrantee information of the top 3 competitors. Bijohn could also He then commands "buy-price", though he could have commanded "buy-ship" depending upon his preference for low price or quickness of delivery. The e-transaction is instantaneous as all of his credit and banking data (along with any other personal information) is completed with cloud computing.

Chapter 5 – Shifting Paradigms

The evolution of human cultures, philosophies, politics and economic systems have not changed over the millennia, as human behaviors continue to reflect primal reactions to environmental stimuli. While people are usually unaware of the reasons why they may feel or react in certain ways to other people, ideas and activities, in general, human DNA has set in place certain behavioral propensities that appear to be universal across national, cultural and ethnic boundaries.

Egocentricity

a. Childhood expenses & perspectives
b. Deep rooted insecurities & traumas
c. Need to validate self through external means
d. Desire for ego-gratification
e. Status of positions of importance, admiration and power
f. Associating with others of elitist status and class
g. Accumulation of material property and wealth
h. Obsessing on fear and/or respect from others
i. Deception, Illusion, Dishonesty, Denial, & Justification
j. Self image
k. Self beliefs
l. Self behavior
m. Justifying others of like mindset and activities
n We-them orientation – devaluation of humanity
o. Public image & deception
p. Open to and welcoming temptation
q. Bribery
r. Kick backs
s. Vices and good time activities
t. Criminality
u. Immorality

Actualizing, recognizing, and investigating corruption

     v.   Opportunism

     w.   Networking

     x.   Secrecy

     y.   Manipulation

Factors That Affect Future Global Development and the Economic Destiny of America

The new millennium was ushered in by a set of new realities, each sharing uncertainty and unpredictability as common factors. This uncertainty paradigm has permeated almost every area of international relations, domestic affairs, and individual lives. How well our leaders, groups, and individuals are able to deal with complex and dynamic problems will determine the future prosperity or demise of America.

We must look at the most pressing and consequential areas of concern, and solve these urgent problems before we pass the point of no return, and cast our combined fates to the wind as reactionary pawns on the global chessboard. We need to recognize who our true friends are, and who our competitors, and potential foes may be.

Political Trends

1.   *U.S. Hegemony on the decline?*

Many MNCs are home-based in Europe, and their ownership of American and foreign corporations has greatly expanded since the 1990's. Increasingly, Americans are finding their paychecks being signed by managers who represent foreign corporations and conglomerates. While the majority of MNCs are owned by Americans, many investor owned, the CEOs who run them receive the greatest disproportionate economic benefits, as stockholders rarely receive their just dividends due to the collusion of elitist Board of Directors who also gain from company profits.

As global opportunities widen abroad, there will be a rise of wealth to foreigners, who as a group will attempt to challenge American economic hegemony by creating regional free trade zones, that will exclude the United States.

2.   *German Hegemonic Goals*

Two world wars were initiated by the Germans, and it was the Germans who defeated the Roman Empire's attempts to expand north. Germans are predisposed to be aggressive and feel superior to other races and ethnic groups. Their history and heredity is filled with violence, and they may be genetically driven to conquer those whom they feel are inferior. Subsequent to the terms of surrender at the end of World War II, the Germans were prohibited from building another formidable military and standing army; however, as a member of NATO, they participate in a modern military and so called self-defense forces. The Germans provide the backbone to the Euro, which has gained 30 percent in value in the past year, compared to the U.S. Dollar. It is the German economy that is driving the economic engine of Europe, and the world's second largest bank, Deutch Bank in addition to Daimler-Chrysler and Mercedes-Benz are all German corporations. As America's final cost to reconstruct Iraq and to wage the War on Terrorism will likely reach a trillion dollars, added to a half trillion dollar deficit, the German-French partnership will prove to be a formidable obstacle that challenges U.S. economic and political interests abroad. If America's economy declines as a result of outsourcing, terrorism, investment scandals, hedge fund attacks, ongoing corporate corruption, and a potential trillion dollar budget deficit, the Euro will continue to gain value against the U.S. dollar, and the Germans stand ready to challenge Americans for the top economic position.

3.   *Demise of Britain's Influence*

Two costly world wars depleted England's treasury to the extent that they willingly gave up essentially all of their colonies on every continent on Earth, from Africa, to India, to the Middle-East, losing the great mineral riches of gold, diamonds, and oil behind. The U.K., the enemy to early American colonies, has subsequently proven herself to be America's most consistent true best friend, who continues to repay her gratitude for American lives shed to save her from German conquest during World War II. Without the riches of her colonies, Britain has experienced a continued slide, both economically and politically on the world stage. Her strength comes from a long history and heritage filled with pride, civility, literature, and philosophy, which by the luck of circumstance complements what America in many respects is losing as a society, primarily due to the high influx of cultures who have non-Anglo values and orientations.

4.   *China's Balancing Act*

In the case of China's economic development, the money-mania and new capitalistic orientation has resulted in a greatly reduced level of anxiety and suspicion between the communist leadership and American leaders. China is now one of America's largest trade partner, and holds almost $300 billion in U.S. bonds and dollars. Their modernization has placed their socialism on the back burner, as both Party members and well-connected entrepreneurs pursue wealth building with a passion.

5.   *Russian Resurgence*

As the Russian economy grows stronger and more stable, Putin has taken on the Jewish oligarchs who picked up Russian assets for pennies when communism collapsed, who then gained control of entire sectors of the Russian economy, including oil and media. When these oligarchs tried to take over the government of Russia, by planning to run candidates against Putin, he put arrest warrants out for the top 3 oligarchs in Russia. One got away, but all lost their financial empires back to the state. The political climate in Russia has always been somewhat treacherous, with changes at the very top brought on by coup de tats, which mirrors the spirit of the Russian revolution. Putin is ex-KGB and knows all about the inner workings of the Russian government, military, intelligence network and is well connected. He keeps his agenda close to his heart and gives few clues about his strategy until he is ready to pounce on his enemies like a jungle smart tiger. Should the U.S. leadership trust him? We have not choice but to communicate and work toward common goals, one of which is to secure all nuclear weapons from terrorists, and to keep them off the black market. During the cold war, decades of tense detente kept U.S. and Soviet ICBMs aimed at major cities in both nations.

Now, with the miniaturization of nukes, it's possible for a secret war of attrition to be waged by selling mini-nukes on the black market. We need to have the cooperation of Putin to prevent nuclear exploitation and extortion. There are economic and trade opportunities, and Iraq could provide a platform for American and Russian leadership to build bridges and more trust on areas of common concern. But we should never be too naive to believe that Russian ICBMs and nuclear submarines can't be retargeted within minutes to cold war settings, in the event the political leadership in Russia changes for the worse in the unpredictable future. Let's hope the leadership in Russia will continue to take the road of partnership and international peace and stability

6.   *Rise of Islamic Extremism*

For the past generation, Arab despots and religious zealots have brainwashed their children to hate America, resulting in the rise of anti-American feelings, the growth of terrorist cells, and inspiring Jihadists. How can America change the minds of haters who have been trained to kill themselves for the promise of an afterlife with 30 virgins? We can't. The downfall of Saddam and the hopeful democratization of Iraq appears to have stimulated Omar Kadafi of Libya to pursue a course to join moderate Arab nations in the world's economic order. North Korea and Iran have recently appeared to be giving signals of a desire to be more cooperative with the international community, the west, and the U.S. We hope the extreme religious leadership that exist in some Arab nations will become more pragmatic and choose to coexist and even to cooperate with the West, but let's not hold our collective breath.

The Arab culture, religious dogma, and male chauvinism still places a high value on strength and devalues niceness. We have seen that Arabs consider themselves to be courageous when they carry out suicide bombings. Westerners think suicide bombers are extremely crazy and mislead. Just as Saddam would order others to blow themselves up, but could not find the mindset to kill himself rather than to be captured; other despots and tyrants in history and those who rule their nation-states with an iron fist respect only strength and a steely resolve. Let's not forget that millions of Arabs already hate us, and have hated us for a generation due to our support of Israel. That's not likely to change. The respect for the iron fist is also not likely to change. So when Islamic zealots and crazies challenge us, let's give them the iron fist, knock them down, and do what we got to do. As for the moderate Arabs and Moslems, we should continue to support efforts to partnership on economic issues and trade, and as much as we can, try to win their hearts and minds. The Arab world will probably never love us, but we could benefit from a lessening of the intensity of hatred.

7.   *Domestic & Global Terrorism*

Every year, over 12 million people are arrested in America, which is roughly 7 percent of its population over 15 years old. Over 2 million people are incarcerated, making the U.S. the largest penal colony in the world, exceeding even China's prison population. Crime statistics show that incarceration makes people into worse criminals, as the recidivism rate exceeds 70 percent because petty criminals learn to become worse criminals in the prison university system. It can be safely presumed that the 3 strikes law encourages third strike felons to turn to more violence and to commit more serious crimes, since the penalty for capture is the same 25 years to life.

Undoubtedly, most graduates of our prisons who are released back into the general civilian population without employable skills, turn again to crime. Any terrorist network would find little resistance hiring ex-felons with a bone to pick with our government and society, as payback for their years of incarceration. Global terrorism will be stopped only after legitimate national governments commit sufficient numbers of soldiers necessary to hunt down all terrorists, their bases and training camps everywhere. As long as nation-states continue to harbor terrorists, they can not be fully neutralized, and will be a threat to civilized nations.

8.   Other Significant Global Actors

There are secret hands attempting to stir up the global stewpot, some independently, and others in as strange bedfellow. Israel, Saudi Arabia, France, MNCs, and oligarchs also seek to influence world events from back door politics. Israel has her agents and political lobbyists hard at work in western nations and developing markets, attempting to get in the middle of large profitable deals, and positioning Jewish brokers as gatekeepers to solidify control over resource distribution and pricing. The Saudis, now recognized as a hotbed of anti-American jihadists, attempts to walk the tightrope between western detente, alliance with the U.S., and placating anti-Semitic Islamic extremists. France hangs on to the German coat tails, and attempts to use Germany as its partner, or backup muscle. MNCs and oligarchs have huge stokeholds in creating a world order that concentrates wealth to a relatively minuscule economic elite. And international Jewry pursue a common vision and path to consolidate their political influence and economic muscle in the four corners of the world. Islamic extremist, jihadists, and terrorists groups work a sympthetic and loosely associated network to disrupt all western interests, especially those of the U.S. and Israel, and increasingly, any ally of America.

9.   Politics of Oil Supply Manipulation

The major global exporters of oil are Saudi Arabia, Kuwait, Qatar, UAE, Russia, Nigeria, Mexico, and Valenzuela, all which accept U.S. dollars in exchange for oil, as America is the world's largest consumer of oil and gas. There appears to be discussions among certain oil producing nations to hedge against the U.S. dollar, by considering switching to the Euro and/or Japanese Yen as the official monetary exchange medium, instead of the dollar. If an effective conspiracy between major oil producer can materialize, de-dollarizing oil exports would force the U.S. to exchange dollars for Euros and Yens to pay for oil imports, which would further weaken the dollar. Fortunately, several of the oil producing nations have positive political relations with the U.S. for now, and would likely not enter into an arrangement that forces the U.S. to take some unpredictable reactionary position. During the Arab oil conspiracies of the 1970s and early 1980s, OPEC, especially Saudi Arabia became filthy rich from manipulation the supply and price of oil. These Arab oil producers became so rich, they could not spend the money fast enough. Saudi Arabia used American banks to help them to invest their hard cash, as Nixon had delinked U.S. currency from gold, the wealthy Arabs had to invest their overabundance of cash somewhere, and the most secure investments appeared to be American. Subsequently, the U.S. dollar plunge in value during the mid to late 1980's and the Arabs, particularly the Saudis saw their net wealth shrink almost in half. It may be possible for oil producers and the Jewish oil brokers to again attempt to control global oil prices again in the future. The U.S. needs to be ready for any contingency, if oil producers should attempt to inflate oil prices while de-dollarizing payment from the U.S.A., which would likely have serious political consequences.

10. Political & Bureaucratic Reform

American politics has become rife with temptation and dependency on special interest groups, who exchange political contributions for a stake in future policies. As lobbyists increase their investment and stake in key politicians, our elected officials worry that removing the stake would certainly cause irreparable hemorrhage, and would become political suicide. The cost of political campaigns, even with election reform laws, has become obscene because politicians realize that the most efficient way to reach potential voters is through television advertisements and ten second sound bytes. The sector who gains the most from political campaign coffers are the national television conglomerates, who already earn over $80 billion annually from advertisers. Political backers don't do anything for nothing; there are no free rides in life. Consequently, elected officials are indebted and essentially bought off by special interest groups, and fell less compelled to represent the diverse and varied interests and viewpoints of any other general public constituency.

Agency chiefs and bureaucratic officials occupy key gate keeping positions, which either prevent or permit policy flexibility and circumvention, or emphasize prosecution. A wealthy political donor is more likely to get that street light in front of their driveway in a safe and protected exclusive community than entire communities who complain about poor lighting that contributes to higher crime. Special interest lobbyist also wine and dine key public administrators, because they are in positions to cut the red tape, to make exceptions to the rules, and to overlook potential violations of various codes, ordinances, procedures, and certain laws within their jurisdiction of enforcement. Influence peddling can become a corruptive enticement for those bureaucrats who feel their pay may not be commensurate with their level of responsibilities, title, and lifestyle needs.

11.   Geo-political Environmental Impact

We humans live on a relatively small planet, when compared to known planets in our solar system (five are larger), such as Venus and Saturn. We share limited space, breath limited air, and drink limited water. As our population continues to explode, our collective human and industrial pollution alone is destroying every aspect of our limited biosphere, while causing massive species extinction on the magnitude of millions of species of plants, animals, fish, and bacteria. Our single homo sapiens sapiens species has single handedly caused the wanton destruction of almost ten million species that had once lived on planet Earth ten thousand years ago, a relatively short geological time.

Nation-states share the world's waterways, oceans, and atmosphere, the actual molecules of which constantly moves across national boundaries and borders. Human beings' need for possession and land ownership has driven civilizations to clash, the world to go to global war, peoples and nations to rise against one another. The history of humanity is one of environmental and cultural destruction on massive levels, that has only continued at an accelerated pace during our modern era. Political jurisdictions and nationalism has carved up the world into destruction zones, with little political will to ameliorate the negative environmental impact of political and economic exploitation.

Economic Trends

The rise of European economic unity appears to have resulted in a new regionalism spearheaded by France and Germany. The Euro continues to gain value against the U.S. dollar, and travelers are able to traverse freely in Europe, even between nations that were traditional enemies. The combined European G.D.P. is making substantial gains against the American G.D.P., for a similar combined population of around 300 million, challenging the U.S. for the top economic spot in the world.

1. Oil & Energy Market Manipulation
2. Stock Market Manipulation
3. Corporate Corruption
4. Effects of Bureaucratic Reform
5. Internet Commerce
6. Corporate Downsizing
7. Unemployment Pandemic
8. Acts of Terrorism
9. Global Oligarchies
10. Multi-National Corporations
11. Off-shore Monetary and Tax Havens
12. Environmental Impact to Global Economy
13. Global Banking System
14. Global Banking Corruption

Social Changes

Along with greater economic and political cooperation, their education system is consistently turning out better educated and functional people, who speak several languages and have a broad worldview that is more tolerant of diversity and cultural differences, than what people typically experience in America.

1. Mass Media Manipulation
2. Educational Deficiencies and Reforms
3. Bifurcation of Economic & Racial Classes
4. Feminist Agenda
5. Racial Politics
6. Political Agenda
7. Civic Capital
8. Privacy & Spying
9. Government Controls & Laws
10. Cloning and Genetic Modifications
11. Exploitation of Cheap Human Capital
12. Mass Refugee Relocation

Military Development

Israel, and European faction of N.A.T.O., in addition to the British possess formidable advanced weapons and WMDs, including nuclear weapons, that in the aggregate, rival the superiority of America and our most advanced systems. Russia has always been a nuclear competitor, as China and smaller nuclear nations pose potential future challenges to American military hegemony.

Already, Israel touts the most advanced surface to air missile (SAM). which they demonstrated in the prestigious 2003 International Paris Air Show, which is the annual showcase for jet planes and related military weapons. The Israelis also boast of their production model tank that is supposedly superior to America's top of the line Abrams tank. The transfer of American military technology through military contracts, subcontracts and espionage has taken away our weapons systems superiority, as our military increasing depend on foreign companies to manufacture and produce key components used in the assemblage of our most modern high tech weapons systems, planes, armor, uniforms and communications gear.

We should no longer assume that America is capable of winning any and all future military conflicts, as our troops and military assets are spread far and wide in the global policing mission and war on international terrorists. Our difficulty in fighting protracted urban insurgency underscores the heavy toll in casualties that 21st century warfare entails, due to block to block fighting. The traditional cut and burn military tactics are not unacceptable to international norms. We can no longer bomb cities, as we did during most previous wars to kill innocent civilians residing in enemy nations. Our troops are forced to shoot only after they've been shot at, or are in imminent danger of attack. This type of warfare places exceptional restraints on our military's ability to execute their missions, and to protect themselves from ambushes and attacks. Furthermore, the international community would likely insist on war crime trials for any general or President who authorizes a nuclear strike on an enemy or perceived enemy, even after a declaration of war exists. Consequently, America is expected to take the first blows by our enemies, then to deliver only a measured defensive response that fails to rid our enemy's ability to wage war or terrorism. This is no way to fight wars! If we must fight any wars at all – and hopefully not more of the false flag escapades, then we must fight to win.

The Geneva Conventions clearly state it's a war crime to deliberately target civilians without regards to their innocence and/or neutrality. Israel and ISIS clearly violate the Geneva Conventions in the type of indiscriminate or deliberate attacks against civilians and other combatants whose rights are covered under the warfare conventions. How First World powers decide to react to war atrocities committed by both ISIS and Israel's IDF will determine the future "morality" of war... as some wars would be viewed as justifiable and moral, when for instance the purpose and scope is to free the enslavement, torture, mass murder, and holocaust of innocent civilians. The free world's war justifications and strategies will set the high or low for human civilizations on its path toward destruction or enlightenment and peace. Let's hope the right choices will be made.

www.ingramcontent.com/pod-product-compliance
Lightning Source LLC
Chambersburg PA
CBHW060246290526
45789CB00001B/208